'Children with autism tend to live in a world of their own, not motivated as much as other children to interact and talk. However, there are activities that can increase motivation to communicate and facilitate social play. This excellent book has 300 of these games and activities that are also great fun for the child and adult. Parents, educators and therapists will regularly consult this book for sound advice and creative ideas. If you are not sure what games to play with a child who has autism, this book will provide you with lots of practical ideas and sound advice.'

> – Tony Attwood, author of *The Complete Guide to Asperger's Syndrome*

'Play is the most successful tool in teaching children in need to develop effective communication skills. *Motivate to Communicate!* is packed with easy-to-implement games and activities that remind communication partners to playfully "squeeze" learning opportunities out of practical, everyday materials and situations. Excellent!'

> – Linda Hodgdon, M.Ed., CCC-SLP, speech
> pathologist and autism consultant

'Simone Griffin has put together a broad array of materials and teaching strategies within *Motivate to Communicate!* Parents and professionals alike will find a delightful range of common objects used in creative ways to promote functional communication by children with autism and related disabilities. The book is well organized and will help readers find numerous suggestions for how to design lessons that promote initiation and expansion of communication skills. A great deal of attention has been built into the activities to promote fun – an important key to fostering communication within ever growing social situations.'

> – Dr Andy Bondy, president and co-founder of
> Pyramid Educational Consultants, Inc.

'A marvellous book, full of practical advice that is based on the best available evidence. Written in a clear manner, free of jargon, and refreshing in its approach to engaging children with ASD in therapy. I am sure it will become a standard reference for parents and clinicians alike.'

> – Peter Szatmari, professor of child psychiatry
> at McMaster University, Canada

Motivate to Communicate!

of related interest

First Steps in Intervention with Your Child with Autism
Frameworks for Communication
Phil Christie, Elizabeth Newson, Wendy Prevezer and Susie Chandler
Illustrated by Pamela Venus
ISBN 978 1 84905 011 1

Art as an Early Intervention Tool for Children with Autism
Nicole Martin
ISBN 978 1 84905 807 0

Small Steps Forward
Using Games and Activities to Help Your Pre-School Child with Special Needs
2nd edition
Sarah Newman
Illustrated by Jeanie Mellersh
ISBN 978 1 84310 693 7

Fun with Messy Play
Ideas and Activities for Children with Special Needs
Tracey Beckerleg
ISBN 978 1 84310 641 8

Motivate to Communicate!

300 Games and Activities for Your Child with Autism

Simone Griffin and Dianne Sandler

Jessica Kingsley Publishers
London and Philadelphia

First published in 2010
by Jessica Kingsley Publishers
116 Pentonville Road
London N1 9JB, UK
and
400 Market Street, Suite 400
Philadelphia, PA 19106, USA

www.jkp.com

Library of Congress Cataloging in Publication Data
Griffin, Simone.
    Motivate to communicate! : 300 games and activities for your child with
autism / Simone Griffin and Dianne Sandler.
        p. cm.
    Includes bibliographical references and index.
    ISBN 978-1-84905-041-8 (pb : alk. paper) 1. Autism in children. 2.
Games. 3. Play therapy. I. Sandler, Dianne. II. Title.
    RJ506.A9G75 2010
    618.92'85882--dc22
                                                2009020604

British Library Cataloguing in Publication Data
A CIP catalogue record for this book is available from the British Library

ISBN 978 1 84905 041 8

Printed and bound in Great Britain by
MPG Books Limited, Cornwall

CONTENTS

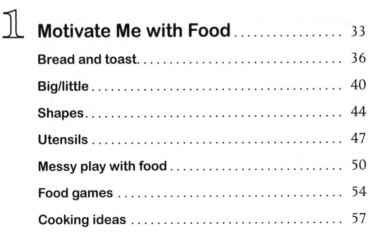

Motivate Me with 'Party Toys'

Motivate Me with Social Games

*'In every job that must be done, there is an element of fun.
You find the fun, and – SNAP – the job's a game!'*
Mary Poppins

ACKNOWLEDGMENTS

FROM SIMONE GRIFFIN

I sincerely thank all the families and children who have allowed me to play and try out all my ideas and toys with them. Many of these ideas have come directly from the children who like to play with things in a 'different' way and also the families that have shared so many ideas with me. I am truly thankful. I would also like to thank the many people I have worked with over the years – they, too, have been generous with sharing their ideas.

I would especially like to thank Colleen Baker for being more than generous with her time and resources in those early years of working which allowed me to explore lots of different toys for the children in the school. I thank Leah Buddle for the enthusiasm she shared with me when searching for all those motivational items and Ruth Harris for her writing support and clinical guidance throughout the whole process of writing this book.

Last, but by no means least, I wish to thank the two boys who inspired me to work in the area of autism in the first place, Sam and Ambrose.

FROM DIANNE SANDLER

I would like to thank all the children and colleagues with whom I have had so much fun over the years. Much of my creativity has come from my experiences in a wide variety of hospitals, schools and nurseries.

I would especially like to thank my colleagues and friends from the early days of my career where we pooled ideas, practised and gave each other much inspiration.

I would like to thank my family (Simon, Joe and Eleanor and Gaye and Roger) who have put up with me bringing my work home, being my 'guinea pigs' and toy testers over the years, and have kept me going.

Simone Griffin and Dianne Sandler will donate all royalites from sales of this book to helping set up a school for children with autism in St. Lucia. For more information about this please contact the authors at motivatetocommunicate@gmail.com.

INTRODUCTION

WHY MOTIVATE?

Well, in the memorable words of Mary Poppins, 'Just a spoonful of sugar helps the medicine go down.' That certainly doesn't just apply to children with autism – we all need motivation…a reason to do something.

Cast your mind back to your own school days. Do you remember a teacher who motivated and inspired you to learn? Remember how this person captured your interest, and made the class seem relevant and exciting. The way they presented their topic made you want to listen and learn, and you obviously remembered it, well after the lesson was over. Maybe this person was key in helping you find your future direction? So, what was on your mind at that point in time?… *Tell me more!*

Compare that positive feeling to the memory of a different teacher – one who stuck in your mind for all the wrong reasons. What is it that you remember? Boring presentation, long meaningless words, dull monotonous voice, lack of relevance to anything? Probably the *last thing* you remember was what the teacher was trying to teach you! What was on your mind then?…*Get me out of here!*

The good news is that you can be that *inspiring teacher* for your child! This book contains over 300 games and activity ideas to help motivate your child, some of which will make your child think… *Tell me more!*

When we talk about motivation, we are really focusing on creating *enthusiasm*, and *interest* in your child, along with a *commitment* to communicating and engaging with you. There is no one formula for this, as not all children like the same things, nor do they like the same thing all the time. Just like the rest of us, they have different preferences, – and it is our job to keep this under review. Through your commitment to expanding and finding new sources of interest for your child, you will find that doors will open for your child to learn new communication skills, and for you both to have the pleasure of sharing new experiences together.

WHO IS THIS BOOK FOR?

The book is suitable for ages 1–100 years! Parents and carers of children with autism were at the front of our minds when writing this book. However, the games and activities presented here will also be a useful resource for teachers and other professionals working with children with autism. We think you will also find that other children with (or without) special educational needs will also enjoy the games and activities. Many of our ideas are also suitable for older students, and family members. Try them out and see!

YOUR CHILD AND AUTISM

We have used the term 'autism' throughout the book to refer to children on the entire spectrum of autistic disorders.

Areas of Impairments

You may well be familiar with the three distinctive behaviours that characterize children with autism:

- Difficulties with verbal and nonverbal communication.
- Difficulties with social interaction.
- Repetitive behaviours or narrow, obsessive interests.

The combination of difficulties in these three areas is what often creates the challenge of developing communication skills in children with autism. However, you can sometimes make the autism characteristics work for you. For example, your child's 'obsessive interests' and enthusiasm for specific things can also be a *huge* strength, because once you have tapped into his or her interests, you have found powerful motivations for your child to communicate with you!

YOUR CHILD'S SENSORY PREFERENCES

All of us are constantly receiving, processing and disregarding a wide range of sensory messages in our daily life. There are the five familiar senses of touch, taste, smell, sight and sound and they all help us to hear things such as a bicycle bell in the distance, feel a gust of wind as it comes through an open door or smell the coffee brewing on the stove (that is *our* favourite!). There are also proprioceptive and vestibular senses[1] that give us a sense of speed, movement and pressure on our bodies and a sense of ourselves in the world.

Most of us can take in all these messages, organize them into the right place and rank their importance to us. Some individuals with autism might have difficulties with these messages and might be considered what we call *hypo-* (under) or *hyper-* (over) sensitive to all of them which, in turn can have a major impact on their ability to focus on an activity or manage their behaviours. By thinking about some of the

---

1   The proprioceptive sense gives us information about how we are moving and where our limbs are in relation to our own bodies. The vestibular sense lets us know whether we are upright, horizontal, moving, or falling, by receiving stimuli from the force of gravity through the receptors in the inner ear.

questions below you might start to get a better idea of your child's sensory preferences.

Children who are *hyper*sensitive might: Tick if applies

- find certain sounds or loud noises distressing ☐
- be sensitive to bright light or particular colours ☐
- find certain tastes or smells repulsive ☐
- have a fear of heights or movement or uneven surfaces ☐
- find certain textures or clothes intolerable next to their skin ☐
- startle easily ☐
- find being close to people difficult. ☐

Children who are *hypo*sensitive might: Tick if applies

- not react to loud or sudden noises ☐
- have a very high pain threshold and therefore not react to being bumped or hurt ☐
- not appear to be aware of the people or things around them ☐
- be unresponsive to unusual tastes or smells (or seek out strong flavours/smells) ☐
- go too close to bright lights or hot items without reacting ☐
- be delayed in their response to events around them. ☐

Being aware of your child's sensory preferences and needs will help you organize the environment and choose the right kind of items/activities to help your child be in the right mood to have fun, interact, engage and communicate with you.

Please note...

Children with autism can sometimes have associated learning difficulties which can impact on how much they understand and learn to do things. Knowing your child's own unique profile of strengths and needs is important for you in order to pitch your activities at the correct level. Talk to the professionals who work with your child for further information and support. For instance, if you are having trouble working out what your child's sensory needs and preferences are you might want to ask your local occupational therapy service for support.

CREATING COMMUNICATION OPPORTUNITIES ACROSS THE DAY

Children with autism communicate at all different levels, some talk, some use sign language, some use pictures to communicate messages and some just reach and point for the things they want. It is important for you to understand your child's communication skills and what you can do to help them. It is not within the scope of this book to talk about all of the great strategies available to help your child to learn to communicate, but we have recommended a few books that might help get you started (see the Useful Reading section at the end of this book). It is also a good idea to regularly talk to your child's teacher and speech and language therapist to problem-solve together about how you might help support your child's communication development.

What we want to help you with is to learn how to motivate your child to *want* to communicate with you across the whole day. Throughout the day, there are endless opportunities that you can create for your child to develop their communication skills. With some thought, it is possible to identify situations in which you can slightly modify the way you behave or slightly modify the environment in order to make more opportunities for your child to practise. You might find that you are missing some opportunities for communication because you understand what your child wants even before they have actually communicated it. For example, a child walks into the kitchen, looks at the fridge and then we say 'Oh, you want a drink of juice.' In this example, we have interpreted what the child wants and have given them the item, without them even having to communicate anything except for looking at the fridge. The following section provides some strategies to help create lots of opportunities for your child to practise their communication skills.

Communication strategies

Out of reach

If your child really likes watching a specific DVD (e.g. Shrek®), place the DVD too high for the child to reach. Your child will then have to communicate with you to get what they want. They can't just put the DVD in and start watching it; they have to point, use their pictures or verbally ask you for what they want.

In containers/jars

If your child really likes grapes, for example, and is able to go to the kitchen and get them whenever they want, then you might like to place them in a plastic container with a tight lid so that they are forced to engage with you and ask for your help before they can get what they want.

Toys that are motivating, have a definite end and are too hard for the child to use by themselves

If your child is having difficulty using a toy by themselves (such as blowing up bubbles/balloons, winding up toys/ spinners, using pop-up toys/music etc.) you might like to try pausing before helping your child with the toy and waiting for them to ask for help, or communicate to you that they need your assistance to make the toy work.

All but one

During daily routines such as getting dressed, try giving your child the clothes that they need to get dressed but miss out something like a sock or shoe so that they have to request the missing item from you.

Bit by bit

If your child really likes cake or playing with a marble run or a Thomas the Tank Engine™ set, instead of giving them all of the items at once, give them some and wait for them to ask for more. You can do this numerous times and create many opportunities for your child to ask for more.

Offer items that the child doesn't want (for 'no')

To encourage your child to communicate 'no' appropriately, offer your child things that you know that they don't like. You could do this at meal time (e.g. ask them if they want brussel sprouts), or ask if they want a DVD that you know that they don't like.

Do something out of routine or unexpected

When you are bathing your child you might like to get creative and ask one of their siblings to get into the bath with their socks still on. This will provide an opportunity for you and your child to comment about 'silly' things.

Hide an item

If your child will only eat fries with ketchup on them – and your child normally goes to the refrigerator to get the ketchup – hide it so that the child has to ask for your help to find it.

Keep quiet

Instead of asking your child what they want to eat when they get to the kitchen you might want to stand in front of the refrigerator/cupboard and say nothing. If your child is really hungry they will indicate that they want something to eat or drink (and then you can respond).

Offer something different

If your child always likes to wear a specific set of pyjamas when they go to bed you could offer something different like a new set of pyjamas (maybe with their favourite character on it e.g. Buzz Lightyear® costume pyjamas).

Creative 'stupidity' (e.g. make mistakes on purpose)

You might like to pretend that you don't know something, or make a mistake 'accidentally' (but you are actually intentionally doing something to get a reaction). This will encourage your child to communicate with you more by either requesting what they want, commenting that you haven't done something correctly or by telling you how to do it. For example, you could pretend to put your child's shoes on and wait for their reaction. You could try to unlock the door with a pencil and leave the keys in your other hand so that your child can tell you what you have done wrong and then what you need to do.

Use opportunities when things go wrong

If your child falls and hurts themselves and they are bleeding, you could ask them what coloured plaster they would like.

Choice making

Instead of always offering your child the same thing (e.g. apple juice) you can create communication opportunities by giving them choices like 'Do you want apple juice, or chocolate milk?' Other examples could include asking questions such as 'Do you want straight Thomas track or curved Thomas track?', 'Do you want smiley face chips or curly fries?'. But remember they don't have to be able to speak to make these choices: you could hold the two choices in front of them and encourage them to point to or reach for the item that they want.

HOW TO USE THIS BOOK

This book contains a wide variety of activities, games and suggestions, some (many, we hope) of which will be motivating for your child. The challenge for you is to find activities that will engage your child. The following questions are designed to help you use this book successfully. A number of activities suggest songs that you and/or your child may enjoy singing. If you are not familiar with any of the songs, you should be able to find the lyrics and tunes on the internet.

There is also a record form in the back of the book (see Appendix 1) which you might also like to use to keep track of what your child likes and what you want to try next time. But to start with, think about the following questions. Some of these questions will make more sense as you read through the book, but try to start thinking about how they apply to your child and you will find that this will help you to think more naturally about how you can motivate your child to communicate.

What does my child love to do?

What does my child like to do when left on their own? What do they like to eat? What are their repetitive interests or habits? Where are their favourite places?

Which activities are similar to what my child already likes?

How can I use a similar item or activity, or use the same item or activity in a different way?

Is there a different activity that I want to try?

Is there another activity or item that you have seen that for some reason you think your child might like?

What time of day is my child most willing to play and communicate with me?

When is my child most alert and happy? When is the best time for me to focus on my child?

How can I make the area where we play as 'friendly' as possible?

What are my child's 'sensory preferences'? How can I reduce potential distractions?

How did the activity go?

How did my child react? What worked well? What could I change for next time? How can I make it easier/harder?

Who can help me adapt the activity for my child?

Do I need help from my child's teacher, a speech and language therapist or an occupational therapist?

Next time I will try...

A shorter play session? A different place? A different activity?
Include another family member? The same again?

SO, I'M READY TO GO...
WHERE DO I SEARCH?

Once you have identified what your child likes and how they like to play and communicate with you then the search begins to find toys, activities and resources that will help you expand and maintain your child's communication skills. Sometimes you can find these things lying around your home. For example, if your child likes to spin toys, walk through your house and try to think of *anything* that could be spun and try this with your child to see if they like it, like putting miniature toys or marbles in the lettuce spinner and getting your child to pull the cord, or teaching your child to flick and spin coins.

It is also important to get other people to help you out with this search as well. Describe what your child likes to friends and family and tell them in detail how your child enjoys certain activities (you might even like to show them so they get a better idea) and see if they can come up with new ideas. They might even have things around their homes which they can share with you to try.

Sometimes, you will need to search for toys in shops like toy stores, party shops, department stores and novelty shops. These are all a good place to start. Discount stores, flea markets and second-hand stores often have great toys and other items that your child will like and at a fraction of the price (and that way you won't get so upset if your child doesn't like a toy that you thought they would like!).

You might also like to try to take your child with you to the shops to see what they are interested in, although we appreciate this is often easier said than done!

Shopping online is another great way to search for new toys and activities. We have produced a list of useful websites that we have found great both for buying toys and also for giving us ideas of what we can make or adapt from toys that we already have. Some of the websites might be international but it is helpful to look at them all as they might give you an idea of the toys which you might be searching for in your home town or country.

Useful websites for buying toys online

www.abilitations.com

A wide range of toys and equipment for children with special needs and links to other useful sites with resources and toys.

www.adaptivechild.com

A range of toys designed and adapted specifically for children with special needs.

www.bakerross.co.uk

Inexpensive toys and craft materials.

www.ebay.com and www.ebay.co.uk

eBay is a great way of locating toys or activities for your child, especially if your child likes to 'spin' and use spin-type toys, etc. When using eBay you will find a good range of private sellers and links to specialist suppliers, where you can look at other items they sell.

www.edenglow.co.uk

Has lots of flashing, spinning and light-up toys.

www.glotime.co.uk

A good site to find lots of slimy, scary, spinning and light-up toys.

www.hawkin.com

Has lots of unusual gadgets, gifts and novelty toys that often appeal to children with autism.

www.integrationscatalog.com

Provides equipment specifically for sensory integration and also has links to other useful sites and articles.

www.jesters.com

Inexpensive toys.

www.ldalearning.com

Provides resources that support a range of educational topics, including special needs.

www.mikeayresdesign.co.uk

This company identifies locations in schools and homes, etc. that can be made into multi-sensory spaces/areas and provides training in how to use them.

www.officeplayground.com

Designed primarily for office workers/executives and sells items such as stress-relieving and fascinating toys, which might also appeal to children with autism.

www.rompa.com

Designs and makes multi-sensory spaces/areas.

www.sensetoys.com

Offers a large range of items, from educational wooden toys for pre-schoolers to games for older children.

www.specialneedstoys.com

A range of toys designed and adapted specifically for children with special needs.

www.thenoveltywarehouse.com

Offers a wide range of multi-sensory resources and toys.

www.tts-group.co.uk

This company has a diverse range of toys and items that might appeal to children with autism.

www.woolgarstoys.co.uk

Offers inexpensive and traditional wooden toys.

Useful websites for creative ideas and activities

www.amazingmoms.com

A useful website which focuses on providing ideas for fun for the whole family.

www.bbc.co.uk/children

This website has lots of different activities, a favourite of which for children with autism (particularly in the UK) is the CBeebies section which has activities, games, printable colouring sheets and stories for you to play with your child and which coincide with the characters and television shows broadcast on the BBC.

www.boohbah.com

An interactive entertainment website specifically designed for pre-schoolers, based on Ragdoll's Boohbah™ television show.

www.crickweb.co.uk

A free-to-use educational interactive resource for primary school children, and also has over 100 links to other free interactive, image and software resources.

www.dotolearn.com

This site provides picture communication cards, songs, games and learning activities and downloadable resources for children with special needs.

www.kneebouncers.com

Choose from games like peek-a-boo or music maker. No experience with computers necessary.

www.mbd2.com

Great website for those who are interested in learning how to make animals out of long balloons as well as other great activity ideas.

www.mudcat.org/kids

This site provides instructions for making your own musical instruments out of resources you can find lying around your own home.

www.oneswitch.org.uk

A website that looks at assistive technology for children who have difficulties activating toys (i.e. need alternative switches, etc.).

www.pbskids.org/zoom

Provides free educational and fun computer games for children.

www.preschoolrainbow.org

Provides a range of ideas for group and circle-time games for preschool children.

www.primarygames.com

Provides games to encourage development in primary curriculum areas.

www.sciencemuseum.org.uk

Provides science experiments for parents and children to try in their own kitchens.

www.skip-hop.co.uk

Provides lots of ideas of songs and rhymes as well as counting and alphabet skipping rhymes for children.

www.thehappyscientist.com

Provides science experiments for parents and children to try in their own kitchens.

www.zefrank.com

A variety of applications and games to play, plus other assorted humour and multimedia.

AND FINALLY...

In the words of Buzz Lightyear (a character in the film 'Toy Story') 'To infinity and beyond!' We wish you good luck and if you come across any exciting and motivational games and toys, please do share them with us on: motivatetocommunicate@ gmail.com.

1
MOTIVATE ME
WITH FOOD

Some children with autism are highly motivated by food. Creating a communication-rich environment around meals, snack time and cooking can help motivate your child to interact with you more and extend their communication skills. In this way your child is improving their communciation skills (which makes *you* happy) and they are doing something that *they* enjoy...eating yummy food!

There are lots of communication opportunities when eating or making food. For example, when preparing food (and this can be as simple as cheese on toast, etc.), you can teach your child to follow multiple-part instructions, such as 'Get the bread out' (part 1) 'and a plate' (part 2). Or you can reverse the roles and get your child to tell you what you need to do in order to make something simple – like making cereal, putting the ingredients into a taco or putting the toppings onto a pizza.

There are plenty of options around food and eating, which means there are countless opportunities for your child to communicate with you and request lots of different items that they want (or don't want!). This might be as simple as holding up two types of fruit and asking your child to point to the one that they want. Or it could involve your child using their PECS folder[1] and sequencing the pictures on the sentence strip and handing it over to you and pointing to the pictures that say 'I want the green apple.' You can also use food to teach the concepts of 'yes' and 'no' by presenting items (items that you know they want and also ones that they don't want) and asking them if they want to eat the item.

---

1   A PECS folder is an interactive folder which children learn to use as a tool for communication. They can exchange a symbol of a desired item from the folder with another person in exchange for that item.

Food can also be a great tool for teaching social skills like sharing and commenting on things that they like or asking family members and friends what they like to eat – and then making that food for them and sharing it with them. For example, your child might ask what toppings their brother wants on their mini pizza and your child could then make a pizza for themselves and one for their brother (with the requested toppings). You can also promote good eating habits and manners with your child, particularly if they are motivated by the end result (something they find yummy!).

Some children with autism have a real aversion to certain foods, but that is okay as you can still teach them to have fun with food and use it as a tool to extend their communication skills. It is important to ask your child if they want to try the food while not putting pressure on them to have it. Also, remember it is always a good idea to eat what you have made in front of the child so they understand what they could do with it. The overall idea is to show that being around food, playing with food and preparing it can be fun and not always a negative experience (and who knows, they might one day like to try what they have made).

BREAD AND TOAST

Children generally love bread and toast and by getting a little bit creative during meal or snack times means you can create lots of different communication opportunities. Remember, it's not always about creating specific 'communication' practice time but rather it's about just trying to incorporate these opportunities into everyday activities.

Things to try

Shapes

By cutting up the toast into different shapes with a knife or cookie cutters you can get your child to ask for the different shapes that they like. You could also arrange the shapes into a picture. For example, a triangle on top of a square could be a house, or lots of circles put together with two thin slices on the front circle to represent antennae could be a caterpillar.

Funny-face toast

There are lots of different toppings which you could use to make a funny face on your toast (depending on what sweet or savoury things your child likes to eat). A few savoury ideas could include: grating cheese, carrot or cucumber for hair; using mini tomatoes or slices of mini cucumber for eyes and making a mouth from a slice of avocado or half a slice of tomato. You might like to put a slice of cheese on to the toast before applying the toppings. If your child likes peanut butter and jam you could spread the toast with peanut butter and then spread eyes, mouth and nose with the jam. The same can be done with a slice of cheese and marmite/vegemite spread on top.

Rainbow

By getting all your spreads out (the sweet ones work best) you can ask your child what flavours or colours they want on their rainbow. You can use square bread, but sometimes round bread looks more realistic. Help your child spread with a knife or to squeeze the spreads from the jar or bottle in the shape of a rainbow – the more spreads, the better the rainbow will look (although not necessarily taste better!). Good spreads to use include: honey (yellow), strawberry/raspberry (pink/red), blueberry jam (blue), cream cheese (white), chocolate spreads/peanut butter (brown). You might also like to teach your child 'The Rainbow Song' as you make your rainbow toast.

Toasties (Toasted sandwiches)

Toasties are a great way to include something different when making a child's lunches, etc. Your child can choose from various spreads and toppings to put in the toastie. When you use cheese in your toastie you can create 'cheese worms' by poking holes in the bread and pressing down on the toast so the 'cheese worms' come through – you could have competitions to see who gets the longest worm.

Jenga™

Jenga is a game that involves stacking wooden blocks into a tower and then trying to remove blocks from within the tower without the tower collapsing. You can play an edible version of Jenga by using toast. First, you will need to cut square toast into 1cm wide strips – you will need at least 20 strips. Once you have your strips of toast you need to build them up into a tower by placing two pieces of toast parallel with about a 1cm gap and then placing the next two pieces parallel on top of the other two pieces but in the opposite direction until you have a tower of toast. The idea behind the game is to pull the strips of toast out (taking turns) without the tower falling over.

Messy toast game

This game is definitely a messy one and is not for everyone. However, it is lots of fun! First, you need to cut the toast into small squares (2cm x 2cm) and then spread various toppings on the small squares. This is where it gets messy, because you then stick the toast squares, using the sticky toppings, to a clean surface such as a window. Next, you blindfold your child with a tea towel and tell them they have to eat the toast off the window and guess what flavour topping they got. If you want this to be less messy you could, instead, stick the toast onto the kitchen bench or a placemat on the table.

Write on toast

You can have lots of fun with letters and words by writing on the toast with various spreads! This is best done by cutting the toast into four or more squares and writing a letter on each square of the toast. You can arrange the toast to spell out easy words for your child to read, make parts of the alphabet or write out your child's name on the little squares of toast!

Balls of bread

When bread is really soft and fresh you can cut the crusts off and place a blob of your favourite topping in the middle (not too much though as this makes it hard to roll!), and roll it into a ball, like a doughnut. You can fill the balls with different toppings and place them in a bowl and guess which topping you think is inside!

BIG/LITTLE

When children start to learn about communication and language they begin by learning the names of things like animals, food and the names of people. After they have started to build up their vocabulary of names (this might be verbally, or though using sign language or pictures to communicate) we need to teach them language concepts such as 'big' and 'little' so that they can follow more specific directions (e.g. 'Bertie, get the little spoon') but also so they can be more specific about what they request (e.g. 'Mummy, I want the *big* sweet'). There are many opportunities and fun things you can do to help your child practise the concepts of big and little and below are just a few ideas.

Things to try

Making big/little

You can have plenty of fun with your child by baking/making big and little foods. For example, you could make cookie dough and ask your child if they want you to cut the cookies out to be big or little. You could also get your child to group the big cookies on one side of the tray and little cookies on the other. You could also do the same with cup cakes, muffins and jelly.

Buying big/little foods

You don't always have to bake foods which are big and little – there are lots of things in the shops that come in different sizes: items like mini toasts, dried apricots and bananas, pizzas, etc. It's a good idea to explore what is available in the shops – you might even want to take your child shopping with you. By having these different-sized items in your cupboards your child will have to be more specific when asking for the items that they want (e.g. 'I want a little apricot'). There is a variety of fun mini vegetables and fruits now available – things like mini potatoes, baby corn, small mushrooms, mini bananas.

Cutlery and crockery

You can be really silly when using different sized cutlery and crockery. For example, when eating soup you could ask if your child wants a tiny spoon (like one from a doll's set) or ask if they want a really big spoon (like a cooking spoon or a ladle). With plates and bowls you can intentionally use things that are too small so that the food doesn't fit in them or cups that are too large for a small amount of drink. Big and little straws are great fun too because if you get a straw that is too small it disappears into the drink!

Party food and treats and sweets

If you're letting your child have treats why not also help them learn the concepts of big/little? There are lots of treats in the shops that come in different sizes, such as Pringles®, Skittles™, M&M's®, Smarties™, cookies, rice cakes, etc. By putting these treats into separate bowls you could play a shopkeeper game, where you take it in turns asking for the treats. Some treats also have different colours so you might ask your child for 'a big red Skittle'.

Quantity

You can also have lots of fun with giving different quantities of food to each other and being silly. For example, you might only pour a tiny amount of milk or juice into their cup if they ask for a small amount. Or you could spoon an enormous pile of mashed potato or macaroni cheese onto their plate if they ask for a *big* amount.

Freezer bag/zip-lock bags

Freezer bags/plastic zip-lock bags come in a range of different sizes and are a great tool for helping your child learn the concept of big and little. For example, you can play a game where you have something in the big bag (e.g. two grapes) and something in the little bag (a cookie), where the child is not allowed to say the name of the food item but only ask if they want the 'little bag' or the 'big bag' – and when they do ask they get to have the item in that bag! The same can be done with big and little containers (you could also put fun non-food items in there too!).

Chopping big and little

Foods that are generally long and thin are also great for helping your child learn big and little (or long and short). So while cutting up the vegetables for dinner you could ask your child if they want big or little pieces of celery, or carrots, and also what size toasts, bread sticks or liquorice, etc. they would like.

SHAPES

Many children with (and without) autism have a keen interest in shapes, and when you start to look around you there are shapes everywhere – particularly when you look at food. You can help extend your child's motivation and communication skills by incorporating fun ideas around two very motivating topics: food and shapes.

Things to try

Cookies

Making cookies is a fun way to explore shapes. You can either use cookie cutters or a knife to cut out the different shapes. You use lots of shapes to make pictures, like lots of stars on top of each other that keep getting smaller to make a tree. Or you could us rectangles and circles to make a person or a flower.

Toast

Toast doesn't always have to be square. By cutting it into different shapes with cookie cutters, knife or scissors you can make toast a lot of fun. You can also put spreads on shapes. For example, you might put the butter on and then squeeze the honey out onto it in a star shape. You can also create toast pictures by putting lots of shapes together.

Cut cake into shapes

Lots of kids love cake! If you make or buy a cake that is fairly flat you can use cookie cutters or a knife to cut it in to different shapes. Or you can have fun decorating the top of the cake with patterns of shapes. An easy way to do this is to cut out paper shapes, place them on top of the cake, and sprinkle icing sugar over the cake so that when you peel back the paper there are different shapes all over the cake.

Crackers

There are lots of different crackers in the shops and these come in many different shapes. You can often get one packet containing a range of different-shaped mini crackers. You can make shape pictures, copy each other's pattern sequences, or separate them into the shape groups. Or you can simply ask each other for lots of different shapes.

Vegetable shapes

Let's face it, some children just don't like vegetables so why not have fun with them and cut them into different shapes? Potatoes are great for this, and if you cut them into thin slices you can use cookie cutters to cut through them to make different shape fries. Another idea is to use scissors to cut out different shapes in lettuce leaves.

Moulding

Some children with autism have a preference for puréed or mushy foods. This can be a great opportunity to have some fun with moulding their food into different shapes. Depending on the texture of their food you might be able to able to cut shapes out with a cookie cutter (e.g. mashed potato is good for that) or use jelly moulds or ice-block moulds (they sometimes come in trays containing different shapes) to put puréed carrot or peas, or rice, etc. in.

Long pasta

By cooking long, thin spaghetti pasta until it is really soft you can have lots of fun playing around with each piece and turning it into different shapes. It is best to place the piece of spaghetti on a surface that has a contrasting colour (like a dark bench or large tray) so that your child can see the pasta better. You might like to have races to see who can mould their piece of pasta into a specific shape or you might like to try to guess which shape they are making. You can also put the shapes together to make pictures.

UTENSILS

Although this section of ideas and activities is called 'fun with food' don't forget that you can create lots of motivation with food by using a variety of different utensils. There is no need to go out and buy new utensils. Most people have one of 'those' drawers in their kitchen that has more utensils in than they know what to do with – well, now you do! And if you don't have many things, I am sure friends will happily donate some of their fun utensils to you to use with your child.

Things to try

Big/little

As mentioned before, you can be really silly when using different-sized utensils. For example, when eating soup you could ask if your child wants a tiny spoon (like one from a doll's set) or ask if they want a really big spoon (like a cooking spoon or a ladle). With plates and bowls you can intentionally use things that are too small so that the food doesn't fit or cups that are too large for a small amount on drink. Big and little straws are great fun too, because if you get a straw that is too small it disappears into the drink!

Straws

There is a large range of different drinking straws and you can often find these in the party sections of shops. Straws can be a lot of fun and they can be really thin, really thick or they can be curly and bendy. Lots of fun can be had by having a few straws to choose from and playing games with sucking up different textured foods and drinks. For example, drinking water, juice and soft drink through a straw is easy – but have you tried sucking up yoghurt or custard?! (You might need to thin it out with milk or water if it is too thick.) Jelly that hasn't fully set is another one to try. You can have races to see who can suck the fluid up the straw the quickest.

Icing bags and paintbrushes

Use icing bags with different nozzles for pushing through food to draw patterns. Alternatively, cutting a small hole in one corner of a freezer or zip-lock bag and filling the bag with food like custard, yoghurt, runny mashed potato (or other runny puréed foods) can be fun. If this is too difficult for your child you might like to use a new paintbrush and spread a thin layer of food on a tray. Then let your child move the food around with the paintbrush as a way of drawing or writing.

Garlic press

If you have an old-fashioned garlic press, lots of fun can be had by putting different foods into it and pushing it through to make lots of 'worms'. For example, cheese works really well when you push it through a garlic press. Soft bread, bananas or raw cookie dough are great for pushing through and making lots of worms. You might like to sing 'Going Down the Garden to Eat Worms' while playing this game.

Forks

Forks are a great tool for drawing patterns in foods like mashed potatoes, ice cream and cakes with icing or cream on top of them. You can also have fun making patterns with forks by pressing them firmly into toast, cakes and bananas, etc.

Scissors

Kitchen scissors are great for cutting food and can be used to practise scissors skills or just to have fun with food. Scissors can be used to help cut pizza into pieces or cut pitta bread into shapes. If you don't want your child using a knife you could get him or her to use scissors instead to help cut the celery or cut bananas into pieces!

Be silly with the wrong utensils

Using the wrong utensil can be a good laugh and/or can encourage lots of communication and discussion! Try giving your child a fork to eat their runny soup, custard or yoghurt. You could also give them a really big spoon for eating their yoghurt – one that doesn't fit into the yoghurt pot. Try giving them a fork to spread something on their toast.

MESSY PLAY WITH FOOD

Messy play can be the source of much enjoyment with many communications opportunities to help your child become more comfortable with new foods – particularly if he or she does not enjoy food or eating. Messy play with food can be a chance to have fun with food without the pressure of having to eat it. It is also a great activity for supporting early communication opportunities such as joint attention, anticipation (like pausing or counting) and hiding items in the mess so he has to find them. A large seed tray from a garden centre or a roasting tray are ideal containers to put the 'mess' in, and having a range of different tools (e.g. spoons, scoops, water/sand wheel,[2] different sized/shaped plastic containers, an egg whisk, funnels and cookie cutters) will make messy play fun for everyone.

Things to try

Cornflour

Cornflour and/or custard powder mixed with warm water in a tray can create some great mess to play with. You can create different textures (depending on the amount of water you add) and manipulate it in many different ways. Sometimes it can go very stiff if you don't add much water, which can make it fun to play with in your hands. You might also like to add food colouring and various scented oils to make it even more interesting. If your child doesn't like

2   A water or sand wheel is a toy where you can pour water or sand into the top of a tower and watch it spin a wheel.

getting their hands messy keep a bowl of clean water close by so they can wash their hands, or provide kitchen gloves for them to put on. You can also use tools such as paintbrushes or containers to manipulate the mess.

Pasta (cooked and uncooked)

Pasta is great to use for messy play because it comes in all different shapes and sizes. You can play with it dry (i.e. uncooked) and sort and match it into shapes, etc. or try to crush or break it with your hands. You can also use cooked pasta, which has a great slimy feeling (and is initially warm) which is great to squeeze through your fingers, cut up with scissors, or manipulate into pictures or letters/numbers. You can also add a bit of oil to it so it becomes a little bit sticky and then you can squeeze and mould it into balls!

'Instant' foods

There are lots of different cheap and easy to find 'instant' foods in the supermarket that make great messy play textures. Things like instant potato mash, jelly, baked beans/tinned spaghetti, custard and rice puddings are all great textures to scoop, mould, squash and mash. You can get really creative by mixing different foods and making messy play landscapes. For example, you can make mashed potato mountains and jelly lakes and use crushed cereal such as shredded wheat for hay or grass on the farm!

Ice 'magic'

Using ice in messy play can make it very interesting and is great fun on a hot summer's day. You will need to make up the different ice shapes (ice cubes and blocks of ice in small containers) the night before – your child might like to help with this too. You can then place all the different ice blocks in the tray and gradually add warm water to watch the ice blocks melt (great for teaching your child the concept of 'waiting', particularly if there is a sweet in the ice that they are waiting for!). By adding food colour to the ice blocks before freezing them and then watching them melt you can create lots of colourful patterns in the tray. You can also sprinkle salt onto the ice to speed up the melting!

Lentils and rice

Different types of lentils, soup mixes and rice can provide some interesting tactile experiences for you and your child. They are often colourful and are great for rolling around on a tray. They are also ideal for pouring from one hand to the other or pouring through a water/sand wheel and watching them spin and spray everywhere.

Salt dribbles

By mixing equal parts of flour, salt and water together you can create some interesting messy play mixtures to paint with in the tray. You might also like to add colour (paint or food dye are good) and pour the mixture into different squeezy bottles so you can make interesting patterns and pictures in the tray. If your child is having trouble squeezing the bottles encourage them to tell you what they want you to draw with the squeezy bottles, or just add some extra water so it is easier for your child to squeeze the mixture though the nozzle.

FOOD GAMES

Food time or meal time doesn't always have to be a routine occasion that is boring for both you and your child. It is important for children to learn early on that food can be fun (and not always a serious thing), as well as a social activity that can be enjoyed by all.

Things to try

Apple bobbing

Apple bobbing is an old game but still a favourite to many children. This is a great game to play outside in warmer weather or simply using the sink or another container in the kitchen. You just need to place small apples into a bowl or tub of water, gently tie your child's hands behind their back and see if they can pick the apple up in their mouth by dunking their head into the bowl of water.

This is a great game to teach your child social rules about games, such as learning not to use their hands, to keep trying (until they get an apple), turn-taking, cheering their friends on, etc. For hygiene reasons it is important to change the water for each child.

Warning! Please be careful to watch all the children during this activity as it does not take long for a child to drown.

The Chocolate Game (with a fork and knife)

The Chocolate Game is a great family or party game to play! To play this game you need a block of chocolate (but don't break it up), a tray, a knife, a fork, a dice and a timer. The idea of the game is to sit in a circle on the floor or around a table. Each person takes a turn in rolling the dice; if someone rolls a six they have one minute on the timer (or longer if they need), to try and cut one piece of chocolate off the block with a knife and fork. If this task is too hard for your child you might need to change the rules a little or help them out. This game only really works if your child likes chocolate!

Eating with *big* gloves

You can play a game similar to the chocolate game where you sit in a circle of friends, with various treats and sweets in wrappers placed in the middle of the circle. If a child rolls a six on the dice then they have one minute on the timer (or more time depending of the abilities of the child) to put the gloves on (these could be washing up gloves or woollen gloves), choose a treat from the bowl, try to open it with the gloves on and then eat it before the timer goes off.

Making food jewellery

Making jewellery with food is fun – and you also get to eat it at the end. Making necklaces with a needle and thread with coloured popcorn is a good one. If your child can't use a needle and thread you can ask them to select the pieces of popcorn that they want you to thread onto the necklace. If you don't want to use a needle, then pasta with holes in it or various breakfast cereals and sweets or savoury snacks that have holes in them are also great for threading cotton or wool into in order to make a food necklace.

Straw games

Straws are great fun, not only for sucking your favourite drink or food up with but also when you play games with blowing. For example, you can play lots of games where you blow and race items across the table. This is great with ping-pong balls but you can also use foods that are light – balls of candy floss/fairy floss, or sweets that are round (like chocolate balls and gum balls). Once the children have blown the food item to the finishing line on the table they then get to eat it.

Guess the food

By playing a game called 'What's in the bag?' you can encourage lots of communication and guessing skills with your child. You might like to hide some of their favourite foods in the bag and let them reach (but not look) into the bag and guess what the food might be. You might like to describe the item (though don't name it) and see if they guess it right.

COOKING IDEAS

Cooking is a great way to have fun with your child and create communication opportunities, but don't be scared off if you are not good at cooking – the more basic the cooking the more your child can participate (even if they aren't very good at stirring, etc. They will find that the more they get to participate the more fun they are going to have). Remember, it's okay to be messy because you can always clean up afterward – and don't forget it is always a good idea to encourage your child to help with the cleaning up. Cooking can be all about the making, not just the end product (we aren't all chefs – and that is okay too). Remember you should always sample the food that you make with your child, because if your child sees you eating what you have created they might be tempted to try it too!

Things to try

Fruit kebabs

By cutting up different fruits into small pieces and putting them into separate bowls you can encourage your child to choose the fruits they like and thread them onto a kebab stick. You can make the experience more motivating by doing the same with sweets/candy (marshmallows work especially well).

Smoothies and ice-cream drinks

Put out a variety of fruits, toppings and ice-cream flavours and encourage your child to pick and choose different combinations in order to make different smoothies. You might like to try small amounts so that your child gets the chance to try lots of different combinations.

Cookies and cutters

Cookie cutters come in all different shapes and sizes (e.g. numbers, animals and geometrical shapes are often favourites for children with autism) and can be used with cookie dough, toast or bread dough to create opportunities for making different choices during cooking.

Ice-cream sodas

For a special treat you might like to try making ice-cream sodas with your child. Put a soft/fizzy drink into a small glass and get your child to put a small scoop of ice cream into the glass and watch it foam up. Try to get your child to drink it quickly with a straw. You get more fizz if the drink is not chilled.

Making dough

Making dough for pizza bases or bread can be a messy but fun experience. By having a bowl each, you can show your child what they need to add/do to make the dough (you can buy pizza base mix – to make it really easy just add water). You can encourage your child to count the spoonfuls that they need to put in or to copy actions such as pouring, stirring, kneading or rolling.

Funny face biscuits

You can decorate plain biscuits with coloured icing pens and sweets or dried fruit and nuts (use the icing as glue) to make eyes, nose, mouth, ears and hair, etc. You might also want to try food items like liquorice, hundreds and thousands (sprinkles), M&Ms, jelly beans, almonds, raisins, etc.

Mini pizzas

By putting lots of different and yummy pizza toppings into separate bowls you can encourage your child to communicate with you and request the toppings they want to put on their pizza (you can use mini English muffins or cut up French stick as your pizza base).

Popcorn

Popcorn can be used to make necklaces and other jewellery (or Christmas decorations) by threading onto cotton – coloured popcorn looks especially great. You can make the popcorn together and get your child to help, either with a popcorn machine, microwave or in a pan. (You can be silly with pan popping by lifting the lid while it is still popping because it jumps out everywhere – your child will love this.)[3]

---

3 Warning! Please be careful and ensure that the hot corn kernels or oil do not burn your child.

MOTIVATE ME WITH
'PARTY TOYS'

There are lots of 'party toys' which children with autism love to play with, bubbles, balloons, pull-back cars, wind-up toys and slinkys being a few of their all-time favourites. These types of toys can be found in discount/cheap stores, the party section of the supermarket or online party stores. However, although generally cheap to buy, these toys unfortunately often don't last long. Many such toys are great for socially interacting with your child. Party toys are good because your child will often need help in order to play with them, which, in turn, forces your child to communicate with you.

To keep up the excitement of these 'party toys', we recommend that you get a special box (with a lid) and label it 'party toys', and then place the box out of reach of your child. This will prevent your child from having free access to them and thus getting bored of them quickly. It will also help your child learn that some toys are only for special occasions, and therefore the excitement of these toys lasts longer. You can also use the 'party toys' as a reinforcement for good behaviours or something to look forward to after coming home from an exciting activity like the park (sometimes it is hard for a child to end something that they are enjoying, like the park, but if you tell them that after the park they can have 'party toys' your child might be able to transition between the activities more easily).

When it is time for 'party toys', get the box out and show your child what is in the box. You might like to talk about each item and describe it as you get it out and then place it back in the box. At this stage, try to hold the box just out of reach of your child (e.g. place it slightly behind you or to your side) so that your child can't just grab at everything in the box. Using a lid helps to control the situation and also helps with teaching your child to play with just one toy at a time.

It is always nice to start 'party time' by giving your child a 'freebie'. In other words, let your child choose what they want by taking an item out of your hand or pointing to the item that they want and not pushing for more formal communication. This will help 'party time' start out on a good note. After they have had some fun with the toy, remove the item so you can encourage your child to use more formal communication, or, in other words, make your child work a little harder to get the item or activity that they want. You might want to help your child learn the concepts of 'up/down' by encouraging them to request using the a verbal sentence 'I want bubbles up,' sequencing their PECS pictures and pointing to the picture that represents 'I want bubbles up,' or by getting your child to point up or down to indicate where they want the bubbles to go.

'Party toys' are fun for everyone and you can also invite other family members and/or children to join in the fun. This will help your child learn turn-taking and sharing and other important social skills.

BUBBLES

Bubbles are a quick and versatile activity that can be used to teach lots of communication skills and targets. For example, communication targets might include language and/or concepts such as 'up/down', 'big/small', 'one/many', 'pop/stomp/clap', 'your turn/my turn', 'blow' and 'counting'.

Things to try

Catch the bubble

By catching the bubble on the wand it gives your child time to look, play and respond to the bubble. Your child might also like to blow the bubble or pop the bubble from the wand.

Big and little bubbles

Blowing the bubbles quickly will give your child lots of little bubbles, and blowing slowly and softly will make the bubbles bigger. Just before blowing the bubbles you can give your child the choice of big or little bubbles.

Wand size/shapes

Bubble wands come in all different shapes and sizes, and although the shape of the wand won't change the shape of the bubble your child might like to choose different shaped, coloured, or sized wands to blow their bubbles from.

Popping, clapping and stomping

You can encourage your child to pop bubbles using different actions. For example, you can pop bubbles with your fingers, or by clapping your hands together, or simply by stomping on them with your feet. You can also get really creative and get your child to pop them with different body parts such as nose, knee, etc.

Bubbles everywhere

You can encourage your child to choose where they want bubbles blown. For example, your child might like the bubbles blown on the door or window (they stay longer), or on different body parts. They might like the tickly feeling when bubbles are blown on their tummy or feet, etc.

Up and down

You can teach your child the concepts of 'up' and 'down' with bubbles. To start with you might blow the bubbles up and say 'bubbles up' and then encourage your child to extend their communication to include both words, and then introduce the concept of 'down'.

Bubble volleyball

You can play bubble volleyball by blowing a bubble and then having two people stand opposite each other and blowing the bubble across from one person to the other until it pops. You can either make a volleyball net by tying a piece of string between two chairs or you can just imagine that the net exists.

Scented bubbles

It is possible to purchase a variety of different bubbles, even scented bubbles! You might encourage your child to ask for different smelling bubbles, or you could play a game where they have to guess what scent the bubble is. It doesn't matter if your child gets it wrong, it is more about teaching your child how to guess.

Counting bubbles

You can help your child learn to count in a fun way by counting the bubbles that you have blown. Remember to count quickly because the bubbles will pop. If your child has difficulty keeping up with the rapid popping bubbles, you might want to try the non-pop/touchable bubble mixture. (Touchable bubbles work just like ordinary bubble blowers – dip the wand and blow the bubbles – but these bubbles harden in the air so they don't pop!)

Things to remember

If your child can't blow bubbles you might want to get bubble wands that are motorized whereby your child only has to press the button. If you have a fan your child can turn on, you can hold up the bubble wand to the fan (or mini fan) and get your child to turn it on.

When bubble mixture lands on hard floors it can be very slippery, so remember to take extra care!

BALLOONS

Balloons are either loved or hated by children with autism. Some children really don't like the squeaky sounds balloons make or are scared of the popping noise that they make when they burst. However, it is good to keep trying to expose your child to balloons even though they might not like them because it is likely that they will come across them at children's parties. Balloons are very versatile and can be lots of fun inside and outdoors. They are great for teaching a range of communication skills and language concepts because your child will more than likely need your help to play with them. The language and communication that might be used when playing with balloons can involve concepts such as 'parts of the face', 'more/bigger', 'up/down', 'colours', 'names of animals' and 'turn-taking'.

Things to try

Blow it up

By blowing a balloon up gradually and pausing and waiting between each breath (with exaggerated facial expressions) you can create opportunities for your child to request more air to be put into the balloon, e.g. 'blow', 'bigger' and 'more'. You can then pinch the tip of the balloon, waiting and encouraging your child to count to three, or say 'Ready, Steady, Go!' (or part of it) and let the balloon fly around the room. If this is too distracting or too noisy you can always hold the balloon and let the air blow on your child's tummy, face or feet.

Balloon buddies

Balloon buddies are a type of balloon that don't burst and that are re-usable (you might need to search online if you can't find them in the party stores). These balloons are great for desensitizing children who are scared of balloons. The balloons are generally made to look like various animals and have legs, tails and faces, etc. You can play lots of games with them by using a pump to blow them up and counting the number of pumps you have to use with your child. You can also pretend that you are feeding the animal (with each pump of air) and watching the animal's tummy grow big. You might like to ask questions around what your child thinks the animals are eating. After the animal is inflated you can either fold in the end of the balloon and throw them around the room or you can pretend that the animal is going to be sick everywhere and let the air out.

Not just air

You can be creative with balloons and fill them with various things like rice, pasta, mini bells or cotton-wool balls. You can then encourage your child to feel, squeeze, throw, or hit the balloons to see what happens.

Rocket balloons and flying saucer balloons

These are a special type of balloon that you can pump up and then let go. The rocket balloons make lots of noise and fly all around the room while the flying saucer balloons fly up and spin around. You can create lots of communication opportunities by getting your child to ask for different colour balloons, or long (rocket) or round (saucer) balloons. You can ask your child to point or tell you where they want the balloon aimed at when it is let go. You can also count down until blast off, and then let the rocket go!

Balloon trampoline

Place a couple of balloons that have been blown up and tied off onto a piece of material. Have two people hold the ends of the material and make the balloons jump up by flicking the material up and down. You can also roll the balloons around on the edge of the material.

Magic balloons

Rubbing an inflated balloon vigorously on your hair or jumper creates static electricity. You can encourage your child to ask you to hold the balloon on their hair while looking into a mirror, to see how their hair stands on end with the static electricity created by the balloon. You can then take turns so your child can see how funny your hair looks when the balloon is held on it. Or you might like to stick the balloon on the wall, door, ceiling and wait for it to drop.

Glove balloons

Some children like to blow up latex gloves as balloons. These can be used with various songs that include fingers/hands and counting. Your child might also be motivated to do balloon 'high fives' or use the balloons in a tickling game.

Balloon people

It can be great fun creating opportunities by playing games and drawing faces on your balloons and turning them into balloon people. You can encourage your child to ask for different parts of the face and, if they are able, you could get them to request different coloured pens to draw on the balloon, or to indicate if they want big or little features. You can also stick wool on the balloon for hair and cut out feet in cardboard, put a small hole in the feet and pull the knot of the balloon through the hole. You can give the balloon people names and pretend that they talk, etc.

Balloon art

Balloon art is where you have long balloons and twist and turn them into something like a dog or a sword. There are lots of websites that explain how to do this – it's not as hard as you think, give it a try and some practice and you will create lots of communication opportunities. If all else fails, you can always draw a face on the end of it and call it a snake or worm!

Helium balloons

Balloons filled with helium can be fascinating and fun for your child. You can sometimes get helium filled balloons from stores that are opening or having a sale – or you might like to go down to a party shop on special occasions and ask if they can fill a few balloons for you! You can create lots of communication opportunities by tying ribbon of varying lengths to the ends of the balloons and getting the children to jump and grab a balloon or ribbon of a specific colour (you could tell them which one to jump for or they could tell you which one they want you to jump for). You can also stick pictures or stickers to the ends of the ribbons to make it more exciting.

Papier mâché balloons

Papier mâché is a great for encouraging communication with your child. If you are not sure how to make papier mâché you can find step-by-step instructions on various internet sites. By cutting out pictures of favourite TV characters, animals or foods from magazines, catalogues and newspapers, and you can name all the pictures as you stick them to the balloon. When the papier mâché is dry you can talk about the pictures that you can see on the balloon – or paint the balloon and turn it into a face or an animal.

Balloon volleyball

Balloons can be used to play an inside game of volleyball. All you need to do is pretend there is a net, and hit the balloon to each other – or you can make a net with a couple of chairs and a piece of string. This game is great for teaching turn-taking and concepts such as 'up', 'high', 'down' or 'low', or pointing to where you are going to hit the balloon next so your child has to follow your pointed instructions.

Things to remember

If you are re-using the balloons or are using the balloons with lots of different children, you might like to purchase a small balloon pump (which can usually be found in discount stores with the water balloons or the long art balloons). This way you won't have different children blowing up the balloons and you won't have to blow them up again after they have landed somewhere not so clean!

If there are little children around it is always important to watch where you leave the balloons, particularly if they have popped, because they can then easily become a choking hazard.

SLINKYS

Slinkys are small columns of tightly coiled wire or plastic which have the ability to move down stairs propelled by their own weight. Slinkys no longer just come in silver (like the good old days!); they now come in an assortment of colours, shapes, lengths and sizes. The plastic ones are easier to untangle and therefore preferable. Slinkys are a great tool for communication and there are many ways to play with them – you just have to think outside the box! Slinkys inevitably get very tangled up with themselves and other toys; it will be important to spend time occasionally untangling them before you start playing with them with your child, so that he or she doesn't become frustrated. Other times, when your child is less excited by the slinky™, you might use this opportunity of a tangled slinky to teach them that sometimes toys are 'broken', 'not available' or 'need fixing'.

Things to try

Traditional slinky games

You can play with the slinkys in the traditional way by putting one end of a slinky on the top of some stairs, putting the other end on the next stair and then letting it go and watching the slinky step down the stairs by itself. Communication opportunities can be created by choosing which step to put the slinky on, counting down (or saying 'Ready, Steady, Go!') and then letting go! You might like to use a digital timer to time how long it takes to come down the stairs, or if you have two or more slinkys you can race them down the stairs to see which one comes first.

Pull and let go!

By getting your child to hold one end of the slinky while you hold the other end you can pull and stretch the slinky so that it becomes really long. You can create communication opportunities by dramatically pausing and counting as you take a step back each time (or your child can ask for 'more' or 'stop') while holding the slinky. When it is fully stretched out you can count down (or say 'Ready, Steady, Go!') and both of you can let go of the slinky and watch it jump and squirm back into its original shape. Alternatively, you could take turns in letting it go and watching the slinky fly back to the other person.

Pull and swing

By getting your child to hold one end of the slinky while you hold the other end you can pull and swing the slinky in all different directions (almost like a skipping-rope action). Your child might like to ask you to swing the slinky up or down or so that it touches the floor, the wall, the ceiling, or to touch a teddy or a friend with their hand out.

Hide the slinky

Slinkys are great for hiding, either somewhere on yourself or around the room, because you can always leave a little bit of slinky showing so that your child can find it! Small slinkys are great for hiding under clothing and when the child finds it they can pull it out and play with it!

Telescope slinky

Slinkys can be used to make pretend (and stretchy) telescopes. By putting one end of the slinky up to your eye and the other end held up to your child's eye you can use it as a telescope and see each other. You can also move backward so the telescope gets longer.

'I Spy' with my slinky eye

Slinkys can be a great tool for teaching your child to play 'I spy'. By putting the slinky up to your eye and then pulling the other end towards another toy or object in the room, your child can learn to follow where the slinky is aimed and guess at what that item might be. This is good for teaching your child to follow eye-gaze or slinky-gaze (a good non-verbal skill that children with autism sometimes have difficulty with). Your child might also like to be the leader and get *you* to guess at what they are looking at too.

Slinky tails and trunks

You can have lots of fun and communication by pretending that the slinky is a tail or trunk of an animal. Your child can choose what animal they want to be and if they want the slinky to be a trunk or tail. You can pretend to be different animals and swing the slinkys from side to side, and pretend to use your trunk to smell different things in the house or the kitchen. You could turn it into an 'I smell a...' activity by putting your trunk up to different food items.

Slinky tunnels

Slinkys make great tunnels, which you can roll balls into and through (ping-pong balls work very well because they bounce nicely through the slinky). By simply laying the slinky on the floor with your child at one end and you at the other end you can throw or flick balls through and watch them fly out the other end.

Things to remember

Slinkys are great fun when you stretch them out and let them go, but it is important to keep the slinkys away from your eyes when they are let go because they can easily fling into your eye or your child's. Take additional care with the metal slinkys as the ends of them are often particularly sharp.

LOTS OF BALLS

Many children with autism like to play with balls but sometimes they will prefer to play with them by themselves. However, by creating exciting games you can entice your child into your games and motivate them to interact and communicate with you.

Things to try

Roll the ball

Sit on the floor opposite your child using your stretched-out legs to contain the ball. Roll the ball to your child, first pausing to encourage requesting. Vary the game with a bounce or throw, etc. This kind of activity will help your child learn turn-taking, waiting and watching the other person as they get ready to throw or roll the ball.

Hide the ball

You can play games with balls by hiding them under a box or cup and getting your child to find them. If you have a few children you might like to have competitions to rush around and see who is the first person to find the balls! Or you can put one theatrically up your or your child's jumper or sleeve and hunt for it together.

Balls through a tube

Use items such as cardboard poster tubes, toilet-paper rolls taped together, or roof guttering to make ramps and tunnels for your child to roll the balls through.

Balls on a tray

By placing a number of small balls on a tray with a good lip (e.g. a cooking/food tray) you can create a game by rolling them on the tray towards your child and encouraging them to roll them back again. You can also make the balls go around and around in the tray or try to stop them in the middle (this is hard!). Tiny Koosh™ balls (soft rubber pompom-like balls) or sparkly pompoms are good for this game too.

Velcro ball and hat glove

If your child is having difficulty learning to catch balls you might like to try Velcro gloves. You can purchase these at toy stores or make them by sticking Velcro onto a glove. Your child might also like the sound that the ball makes when you pull the ball off the glove – but take care they don't fly into your child's eye.

Ping-pong balls

Ping-pong balls can be lots of fun. You can blow them across a table using drinking straws to make them move fast or slow, or you can turn it into a race. You can put them in a bowl of water and fish for them with tea strainers and count how many you catch. Or you can hold them down in the bath and let them go quickly so that they fly out of the water – but take care that they don't fly into your child's eye.

Balls in a bucket

Many children with autism like to throw balls and this can be extended easily into a game whereby your child has to try to throw the balls into a bucket. If you have different coloured balls and buckets you might like to try throwing the balls into the matching coloured bucket. You could make this game harder or easier by holding the bucket and moving it around so your child has to follow where you have moved it to (or if your child has difficulty getting the ball into the bucket you could move it quickly so that the balls land in the bucket). Concepts such as 'high' and 'low' and 'roll' or 'throw' can also be introduced into this game.

Koosh, textured and light-up balls

If your child is not motivated by normal balls there are lots of different 'types' of balls in toy stores and online that you can try. For example, your child might like balls that have lots of fun features, such as lights, squeezable, sounds, dangly parts (such as Koosh balls).

Things to remember

When using balls with your child, please be careful of their size and the age of your child as some of them have the potential to look like sweets or gumballs and could be a choking hazard.

CARS

There are many children with autism who have a special interest in cars. Sometimes, your child might play obsessively with cars and not really involve anyone else in their play or they may just like to spin the car wheels for long periods of time. By creating exciting games you can entice your child into playing with you and motivate them to interact and communicate.

Things to try

Pull-back cars

Pull-back cars are the kind that wind up when you pull them back and race forwards when you let them go. These can be found in most toy stores and party sections of the supermarket. These cars can create lots of communication opportunities, for example, you can pull them back and hold them and count down (or say 'Ready, Steady, Go!') and let them go. You can measure how far they went, or race them to see who wins. You can also teach your child to communicate 'stop' when the car starts to make the clicking sound to indicate that it is wound up and ready to go.

Car hunt

If your child really likes cars and has lots of them already you could set up a car hunt where your child has to close their eyes (or go into another room) while you hide them all around the room or house. Then ask them to run around and find them all and put them in a bucket. (You might tell your child that you have hidden six cars and they have to count to see if they have found them all.) Or, you can get your child to guess where you might have hidden them by verbally asking 'Is there a car under the cushion?' or by pointing to various things in the room and getting your child to look under them to see if there is a car This is good for teaching the 'yes/no' response.

Crash the cars

Generally, children love to make things crash together, and the same applies to children with autism and cars. By crashing toys together you can teach your child actions/verbs like 'crash' and 'fast' and comments like 'oh, no!'

Car ramps

You can have lots of fun by making ramps out of various materials you have around the house and racing the cars down the ramp. You might like to try using trays, scrap pieces of wood or guttering to make ramps. These provide further communication opportunities by holding the cars at the top and counting down (or saying 'Ready, Steady, Go!') before letting them go.

Line them up

Some children with autism like to line cars up. You can extend this to include measuring how long the row of cars is when they are lined up, or you can draw a squiggly chalk line or place a piece of string that your child has to follow when lining the cars up. You might also encourage your child to line them up in colour patterns, like putting all the red cars first and then the green, etc.

Remote-control cars

Remote-control cars can be lots of fun! You can either let your child use the controls or your child can tell you where they want the car to go (while you use the controller). The car can be used to chase or hide around the room, or by drawing chalk lines you can encourage your child to try to move the car on or between the lines. By using ping-pong balls with a remote-control car you can play games where the car has to try to push the ball across a finish line (this is a hard but fun game!).

WIND-UP TOYS

Wind-up toys are a great tool for supporting your child's communication because your child will often need your help to activate the toy! Many of you will be familiar with the traditional wind-up chatter teeth or jumping eyeball with feet, but now hundreds of different, reasonably priced wind-up toys are available from party stores or online. These wind-up toys have also become more technical and can do flips (like flipping monkeys, bunnies and kangaroos) or can roll over (like rolling ladybirds and rolling aeroplanes). Many wind-up toys are relatively fragile so we recommend that you wind the toys up and then put them on the table in front of your child. You might take this opportunity to teach your child to keep their hands on the table and not to touch the toys (only look!).

Things to try

Count the winding turns

Once your child has chosen which wind-up toy they would like, you can ask them to choose how many winding turns you should give the toy. For example, you might ask your child to choose from two, four or six winds. As you complete each wind you can wait for your child to say the next number before winding the toy again. If your child is able to wind the toy you might take turns in winding – this is a difficult skill because you have to hand the toy over and stop the toy from being activated, but if it *does* activate you can then start the counting process again (this will teach persistence)!

Describe it, then wind it!

If your child is learning how to describe things and to use different verbs and adjectives you might play a game whereby you line up a few wind-up toys on the table and get your child to describe two or three characteristics of each toy they want you to wind up (e.g. instead of naming the toys). For example, you might encourage your child to tell you what the main colour of the toy is and whether it has two hands/ feet, etc. or if it jumps, runs or rolls.

Find the same/similar

By putting a few wind-up toys on the table you can encourage your child to find similarities in the toys before they get to wind them up. For example, you might ask your child to find two items that have pink on them, or you might ask them to find the two toys that have feet, or the two that flip over. This will help refine their listening skills, while getting the enjoyment of the wind-up toys at the end of each turn.

'Ready, Steady, Go!'

You can play a simple game where you wind the toy up and hold it until your child counts down or says 'Ready, Steady, Go!' or names the toy. This can be more fun if you wind up multiple toys, hold them all and then wait for your child to name them all and then let them all go at the same time.

Treasure hunt

You can set up a treasure hunt with the wind-up toys where your child has to close their eyes (or go into another room) while you hide the toys all around the room/house. They have to run around and find all the toys and put them in a bucket. You might tell your child that you have hidden four wind-up toys and they have to count to see if they have found them all. You could ask your child to guess where you might have hidden them by verbally asking 'Is there a toy under the cushion?' or by pointing to various things in the room and asking your child to look under them to see if there is a toy there (this is good for teaching the 'yes/no' response).

Race them

Some wind-up toys walk, crawl, jump and run. By lining them up all together in a line you can race them and see which one gets to the finish line first. This is great for teaching the concepts of 'winning and losing' and 'first, second, third, etc.'

MAGNETIC TOYS

Children with autism often like toys with magnetic parts to them. These include things like magnetic numbers and letters, magnetic balls and sticks, magnetic wands and magnetic fishing lines. You can buy some of these toys but you can also make some of them by attaching some sticky magnetic strip and paper clips to photos or small toys.

Things to try

Magnetic sticks and balls

This toy often comes in a tin with lots of different-sized metal marbles/balls and different coloured and sized magnetic sticks. You can create lots of communication opportunities by holding the tin and getting your child to individually ask for the different balls and sticks by colour/size. You can also encourage your child to build them into sequences or pictures (2-D or 3-D) or get them to copy a picture that you have made with the sticks and balls.

Geo magnets

These are magnets that come in all shapes, sizes and colours and can be made into lots of patterns and/or pictures (e.g. pictures of cars, flowers, or people). This is an opportunity to stimulate communication by asking what pictures your child would like to make or what shapes they want to play with. You can support more independent play by tracing around the shapes onto a piece of paper (which could be a picture) and then your child has to find the shapes that match the tracings and build the picture on the paper.

Magnetic marbles

Magnetic marbles can be used like traditional marbles, with the added fascination that they stick together! You can create communication opportunities by getting your child to request how many they want or what colours they would like. Magnetic marbles are fun to drop through cardboard tubes or race down half pipes because sometimes they stick together and move more slowly (which makes the race more interesting), while other times they stay separated and roll down and win the race.

Magnetic wands and fishing lines

You can buy magnetic wands from toy stores or you can simply make a fishing rod with a piece of cylindrical wood, tie some string to it and attach a magnet at the end. You can walk around the house with the wand or fishing rod and test out what it will stick to. You might like to play a game with flash cards or pictures cut out from a catalogue and place paper clips to the cards/pictures and go fishing to see what picture your fishing line can pick up (this is good for helping your child name and describe items or put them into categories like 'food' versus 'animals').

Buzz magnets

These are special oval magnets which come in a pack of two and which are finely polished and high powered. You can toss each magnet into the air and they will create a buzzing sound as they connect together. You can also put one magnet on top of a table and move it around by holding the other magnet underneath.

These magnets are very powerful and should not be placed near electrical equipment such as televisions, computers or digital cameras.

Magnetic art

There are special packs of magnetic toys that come with a magnetic base and different metal items to build on top of the base, such as ocean animals, zoo animals, butterflies, garden items, etc. You can create lots of communication opportunities by giving your child the magnetic base and getting them to individually request the items that they want to build onto the base.

Magnetic letters and numbers

Some children with autism have a special interest in letters and numbers. You can use magnetic numbers and letters to extend this interest and to create words, etc. on the fridge or other magnetic surfaces around the house. The numbers and letters often come in tubs with different colours and sizes (and some capital and small letters). You can create communication opportunities by simply withholding the tub and getting your child to request which numbers or letters they want. It is sometimes fun to give them the wrong one and see if they can communicate to you that you need to get the correct one.

SPINNING TOYS

Children with autism often like toys that spin, like spinning tops, pull-cord spinners or spinning helicopter toys. You can find these by searching online and typing in key words like 'sensory toys', 'spinning toys' and 'autism toys'. These toys are a great tool for supporting your child's communication because your child will often need your help to make the toy spin, or you can get them to ask for different parts of the spinning toy.

Things to try

Counting/timing the spinner

You can encourage lots of communication when using spinning toys with your child by counting how long the spinner stays in the air or trying to count how many spins it does (good luck with this one!). You can count the time for spinning tops, spinning helicopters, spinning balloons, etc.

Putting on different surfaces

By putting a spinning top onto different surfaces it can make different noises and patterns. For example, you might like to put it on a flat ceramic plate, or a cooking tray, lay some aluminium foil in the tray and see what it sounds like, or you might like to sprinkle a little bit of flour in the tray to see if the spinner leaves some patterns. Sprinkles (also known as hundreds and thousands) are also great to put into the tray because when the spinner hits them they fly everywhere.

Putting it on a tray and moving the tray

You can have lots of fun by putting a spinning top on a baking tray, picking up the tray and making the spinner move around the tray. If you can make the spinner spin fast enough you can also flick the tray up (keep holding the tray, though) so the spinner flies into the air and then catch it back on the tray again. You can use different language concepts with your child like 'up', 'flick' and 'catch it'.

Crashing spinners

By placing multiple spinning tops in a tray or flat container lid you can make them crash into each other. You can encourage communication by getting your child to choose the colour spinner that they want and talking about whose spinner lasted the longest and which spinners crashed into each other.

Flying saucer (spinning) balloons

These are a special type of balloon which you can pump up and let go and they spin around. This can stimulate communication opportunities by getting your child to request different coloured balloons. Alternatively, your child can tell you which direction they want the balloon aimed when you let it go. You can also count the amount of pumps of air they want in their balloon or count down until blast off, when you let the flying saucer go!

Helicopter toys

These toys generally consist of multiple parts that include the 'blades' or the top of the helicopter and something to launch it from like a spiral stick or a handle with a pull-string/cord. These toys are great for creating communication opportunities such as counting down to 'launch off' or asking your child where they want the helicopter to fly (e.g. 'under the table' or 'over the table'). You could also introduce concepts like 'push' (button) and 'pull' (cord) to help launch the helicopter.

Spinning tops

Spinning tops come in all shapes and sizes. Some of them you have to push down a spiral pole to make the spinner go; some you might have to pull a cord through the toy to make it spin, or twist a handle on the top and press a button to release the spinning top; others need you to wind some string around the spinner and pull the string. All these different types of spinners create lots of communication opportunities around words such as 'push', 'pull', 'twist', 'press' and 'wind'. Some of the spinners come in packets that have multiple spinners that get smaller in size and you can spin them on top of each other. You could add language to these spinners like 'little' or 'big' spinner and 'top' and 'bottom'.

VIBRATING TOYS

Children with autism are often very tactile and enjoy toys that vibrate. These toys can come in the form of small animals with pull strings, bumble balls, vibrating cushions, hand-held massagers, vibrating teethers, vibrating snakes, etc. These are generally found at special-needs specific stores or online shops. You might also like to ask an occupational therapist about where to locate some of these items.

Things to try

Hide 'n' seek

You can play a game of hide 'n' seek with the vibrating toys by encouraging your child to close their eyes while you hide the toy and then asking them to try to follow the sounds in order to find the toy. Initially, you might just like to hide it under a couple of teddies in front of them so they can see which teddy is moving. You could then hide it under different coloured flannels and play a guessing game as to which colour it is under.

Body parts

You can place the vibrating toys on various parts of your child's body. There are numerous communication opportunities for your child, for example, you might ask your child to follow an instruction like 'Put the buzzy bee on my knee' or alternatively your child could say where they want you to put it: 'I want buzzy bee on my feet.'

Different surfaces

By putting vibrating toys onto different surfaces you can create lots of different noises and patterns. For example, you might like to lay some aluminium foil on a baking tray and put the toy on that to see what this sounds like, or wrap it up in some cellophane or newspaper. You can also sprinkle a little bit of flour in the tray, or some sprinkles (hundreds and thousands), and place the vibrating toy under the tray and watch the flour or sprinkles jump into the air.

Pass the Parcel

You have to be a quick wrapper for this game, but if you can turn a vibrating toy on and wrap it up quickly in newspaper, you can play a fun game of Pass the Parcel and watch how the parcels moves. You can count with your child how many pieces of paper they have to take off. This is also a great game for learning social skills such as listening for the music to stop, turn-taking and following instructions (e.g. only unwrapping one piece of paper per turn).

Light chaser/light spinner

Some toys are not specifically designed to be 'vibrating toys' but include an element of vibration. For example, the light chaser/light spinner is often a favourite with children with autism who like vibrating toys because when the toy spins it also vibrates down the handle. This is a great toy to play with under a blanket, in the dark or under an emergency blanket (as described under 'Light-up Toys' in this chapter).

Bumble ball catch

Bumble balls are hard plastic balls with large bumps all over them. When you switch it on it has a powerful vibration, which makes the ball hard to hold. You can try to play catch or hot potato with the ball with your child and count how many catches and throws you can both manage before dropping it.

LIGHT-UP TOYS

Children with autism can be very sensory orientated and therefore get great pleasure out of different types of lights and light-up toys. Just remember to have lots of batteries ready to go, because if your child likes lights you will inevitably get through lots. It might be better to invest in some rechargeable batteries or wind-up torches!

Things to try

Mirrors and lights

By setting a few mirrors or simply by having a hand-held mirror up you can experiment with changing the direction of light from torches. This is a fun game to play in the dark!

Cellophane lights

By having a couple of torches, some squares of coloured cellophane and some scissors and sticky tape you can create lots of communication opportunities simply by getting your child to request different colours and putting them over the torch and turning it on (you can also project it at the wall to see the different colours). You can experiment with mixing cellophane and seeing what colours you get, and you can also cut out shapes in the cellophane to get some fun contrasts.

Fun with material and torches

You can have lots of fun with your child and create communication opportunities by putting different materials over a hand-held torch. You can move the torch around under the material while your child tries to chase the light with their finger or with another torch from the other side.

Emergency blanket

Emergency blankets can be purchased from most pharmacies or hiking stores and look like a giant piece of strong aluminium foil. You can have some 'disco' fun by getting under the emergency blanket with your child and flashing torches around under them. The light reflects off the blanket and creates a disco atmosphere (this is also a great time to sing with your child). You might also like to take a light spinner/light chaser with you under the emergency blanket.

Tent light chasey

Tents are great to play in with torches because the tent creates a dark room and makes the torches more fun. By having two hand-held torches, one for you and one for your child, you can play torch or light chasey in the tent. You just need to follow each other's lights and try not to be caught – which can be lots of fun. You can attach rules to the game and make one person the 'chaser' and the other person the one being chased – this is good for starting to teach your child social games rules likes this because they will need similar skills in the playground.

Finger and head lamps

There are lots of different types of torches that you can buy. For example, there are head torches that go around your head (these can be found in most hiking/ camping stores) which are great for playing chase in the house in the dark or reading under the blanket, etc. There are also finger torches (small torches with elastic that go around your fingers) that come in all different colours. Finger torches are great for playing light chasey and also encouraging your child to point to the words that you or they are reading from a book. For each page you read, your child could request a different-coloured finger torch (this can be a way to motivate children to read books).

Projection torches

There are many books on the market that also have projection torches with picture discs. These are great for communicating with your child because you can ask your child to talk about what is in the picture or get them to request the next picture. You could also get your child to ask for the projection to be in different parts of the house, for example your child might request 'I want Thomas the Tank on the fridge' or 'I want Thomas on the floor,' etc.

Shadow hand friends

By projecting a spotlight behind you while you and your child sit facing a wall you can have lots of fun making shapes and animals by manipulating your hands and fingers. There are lots of communication opportunities to be had, with your child requesting different animals (e.g. dog, snake, rabbit) and also different actions (e.g. 'make the rabbit jump'). You could also role play and tell stories or get favourite toys and teddies and include them in the 'shadow show'.

STRETCHY AND SQUISHY TOYS

There are lots of toys with stretchy and squishy properties available now in the shops and online. Using search terms such as 'autism toys', 'stretchy toys' or 'squishy toys' will get you some interesting toys to start with. Your child will want to play with you with stretchy and squishy toys because toys are much more fun when you can pull them and stretch them with someone!

Things to try

Stretchy string/elastic

You can have lots of fun with stretchy string or elastic by pulling on one end and getting your child to pull on the other end. You can encourage communication by counting how many steps you can take back before the string is tight, or count down (or say 'Ready, Steady, Go!') until you both let it go at the same time and watch it fly up in the air or make a fun 'ping' sound. You can change your positions when holding the string so that it flies in all different directions. For example, your child might hold it on the floor while you stretch it up high (if your child lets go first then the string should fly towards the ceiling). You can also use stretchy string to make letters, number and shapes.

Warning! Be careful that the elastic does not fly into your child's face.

Catapulting toys

By tying stretchy material tightly between two stationary objects you can make a catapult. There is lots of fun to be had with a catapult by getting your child's favourite teddies, cars and miniature toys, and sending them flying across the other side of the room. You can play games with seeing how high or how far you get them or you could draw a target on a wall and see if you can hit it.

Stretchy test

You can tie lots of different stretchy strings and materials to a stationary object (e.g. a heavy chair) and pull on each one and see how far it stretches. You can make a game of this to see who is the strongest and who can pull it the furthest (put a sticker dot on the floor to mark where you and your child were able to pull each material to).

Twist and twirl

Place two pencils at either end of an elastic band and twist them in opposite directions until the elastic band is twisted tight. You can then count down and let the pencils go and they will twist and twirl all over the place. This game is great for teaching your child verbs such as 'twist' and also counting down or 'Ready, Steady, Go!' You can also do the same with small toys (e.g. people or animals) and spoons, etc.

Fidget toys

Fidget toys are toys that can be 'fiddled with', and are often stretchy. They are also often sold as 'executive stress toys'. A lot of children with autism enjoy playing with these toys. You can get a lot of these toys at the discount stores, at party stores or by asking your occupational therapist or speech and language therapist. Sometimes holding an item such as a squishy ball or a stress ball can help a child concentrate on other things or help with stress and anxiety. For example, it can sometimes be really helpful to have a snap-lock bag in your handbag so that when your child looks like they might be getting stressed you can offer them this as a fidget toy to help them calm down.

Squishy halloween/gory balls

There are lots of fun Halloween and gory squishy balls. These are generally balls with fluid/gel and fake body parts, or insects, etc. inside them. These are great fun to play with your child as you can get them to choose different colours or tell you what is inside when you squeeze the ball.

MOTIVATE ME WITH SOCIAL GAMES

Children with autism often have difficulties socializing with adults and other children so it is important for us to create lots of opportunities to teach our children how to communicate with others and also that they *can* have fun in social situations.

With a little bit of thought and planning, you can gradually introduce more and more people into your child's play, and before you know it they will be developing new social skills as well as enjoying themselves. To motivate your child to socialize, start out intially with something that they already like and are confident and good at (try not to start socializing with toys or activities that they are 'obesessed' with because this often can cause problems – particularly if they have to share the item).

You might also like to practise skills that they might need before other people come over to play with them. For example, if you want your child to learn how to play Pass the Parcel, you might get a couple of teddy bears and sit them in a circle with your child, and practise the skills of passing the present on until the music stops (e.g. you take teddy's turn by helping him to pass it.). Then, when you think your child is ready you might introduce another child (maybe an older child or a sibling) to whom you might explain that they might have to wait a bit longer for your child to pass the present on, or that they might in fact need to *help* your child pass it to them.

Through creating many opportunities for your child to access lots of social play you can help them to learn the skills they will need throughout life, such as sharing, building friendships, problem-solving, waiting, turn-taking, etc.

MUSICAL TOYS

A lot of children with autism like music and enjoy instruments and toys with music and sounds. Musical toys have the advantage that they are often hands-on (i.e. they incorporate cause and effect), so your child gets to participate actively in the play while enjoying the music and sounds at the same time. Musical toys are great for teaching social skills, turn-taking and imitating various rhythms and actions (this could be something as simple as shaking a maraca or banging a drum).

Things to try

Percussion instruments

Percussion instruments are a great way to create communication opportunities. By putting lots of different instruments, or just household items that you can pretend are instruments, into a box (you can often find fun things in the kitchen) you can get your child to request different instruments by pointing to them, using their name or trying to describe what sound they make or what they look like. Another fun thing to try is playing a rhythm on an instrument and getting your child to copy it (or attempt to). Try to think laterally and play with the instrument in different ways, for example, you can bang the drum with your feet or your elbow.

Play it back! (e.g. on a tape-recorder)

A lot of fun can be had with just a simple hand-held tape-recorder/dictaphone or the play-and-record feature on computers/cell phones. Children love to hear recordings of themselves played back. You can create communication opportunities by singing a favourite song into the tape-recorder and playing it back, or you might like to feed your children lines from a book (in short sentences) and then they repeat them after you while they are being recorded. Then when you put it all together it is like an audio book but with your child's voice. Or your child might simply like to make sounds to the book (e.g. animal sounds, etc.).

Microphones

Real microphones attached to speakers, toy microphones (the echoing ones that you can pick up from the discount stores), or just pretend microphones are a great way to motivate your child to talk, sing or just make some fun noises. The microphone is a great prompt that helps your child learn that when they have it in their hands and/or near their mouth it is their turn to make some sounds! You might like to sing part of a song into the microphone and then hand it over for your child to sing or have a microphone each and sing and make noises together. You might also like to try using a microphone when reading a familiar book so you can read and your child can make the noises (e.g. using a book about Old McDonald's Farm) or say the parts that they know.

Make your own instruments

You can have lots of fun with your child by ma
your own instruments. This can be as simple as pu
lentils into an empty plastic bottle and shaking
tying metal bottle tops to a stick and shaking it.
might also like to try making a drum kit by tur
plastic containers or pots upside down and hit
them with sticks/chopsticks or cutlery. Cymbals
also be made with saucepan lids; basically anytl
that makes a noise can be turned into an instrum
By using a box to put your 'instruments' in you
control when your child has 'music time' – otherv
you might find that they make noise all day long!

Music TV and dance shows

There are lots of fun TV shows, DVDs, and comp
games that you can play with your child to l
them learn basic musical or dance skills. These
be enjoyed together, where you can follow what
characters are doing and try imitating it with y
child. You might even like to pause it, and practis
a little more and talk about what you are doing.

MOVEMENT GAMES

A lot of children with autism are constantly on the go and love to move and run around. There are lots of fun movement games whereby you and your child can both run around and also include lots of communication opportunities. Remember, use your child's motivation for movement and get them to communicate about it – that might be requesting movement activities, commenting about the movement or just simply allowing for practice of turn-taking, social skills and following simple directions.

Things to try

Chase and tag

Children with autism often enjoy playing chase and hide 'n' seek games. You can create lots of opportunities for communication and social/play skill development by introducing a little bit of structure into these games. For example, when playing chase at home you might introduce a rule that the person who is chasing needs to sit on a 'cushion' and count to ten before chasing the other person (i.e. to give them time to get a head start!), or you might have a special hat that the person chasing has to wear so that your child understands who is doing the chasing and who is running away. You might also like to tie loose ribbons on to your and your child's clothing, with the idea of chasing each other and eventually pulling off all the ribbons.

Running races

If your child likes to run, you can create lots of opportunities for learning such as following directions, following rules and understanding social concepts such as winning and losing and how to be a good sportsperson. For example, you can teach your child that they need to wait for the 'Go' in 'Ready, Steady, Go' before running. You can then make up races that are more difficult by getting them to follow directions such as, 'Run towards the tree,' 'Touch the tree,' 'Do five jumps and then run backwards back to the house.' You might also like to have running races and write up the results in chalk on the pavement, teaching them that they will win some races and lose others but that the important thing is to try again and that they had fun!

Handstands and wheelbarrows

Some children with autism really enjoy being upside down. You can turn this into a game and create lots of communication opportunities for choice making and counting, etc. For example, you might like to get your child to choose if they want assistance with doing handstands (whereby you hold your child up straight in the air by their ankles while they have their hands on the ground) or wheelbarrows (where you hold your child's legs while they walk on their hands on the ground). You might also like to count how long they are on their hands or how many steps they take with their hands.

Clapping games

Clapping games, slapping games and banging body parts can be fun games with your child and can teach them to follow directions while they socially interact with you. For example, you might clap your hands in a simple rhythm and get your child to do the same. You can gradually make it more complex by clapping your hands, stomping your feet and touching various body parts in a particular order and encouraging your child to do the same. You might also like to encourage your child to tell you what you are doing as you do it, e.g. 'Daddy clapping, Daddy stomping, Daddy touching his nose'.

Dizzies and human helicopters

Many children with autism like to spin and if your child is light enough in weight and you can pick them up, you can play fun games like 'dizzies' or human helicopters, creating lots of opportunities to request more of the game. For example, your child might like to request a 'back dizzy' or 'back helicopter' whereby you hold your child under their arms with their back towards you and spin around quickly so their feet fly off the ground. You might like to try a 'forward dizzy' or 'forward helicopter' which is the same except that your child faces you when you do this. If you are really careful, instead of holding your child under the arms you can spin them around by their legs (making sure there is a soft landing) or you might like to alternate holding their left leg and left arm. Lots of choices for your child!

Blanket swing

Many children with autism particularly enjoy going on the swing at the park. You can recreate the swinging action in fun games at home or in the classroom whereby you get your child (if they are light enough) to lie in a blanket and have two adults, each holding one end of the blanket, picking it up and swinging it. This provides lots of communication opportunities for requesting more, or big and little swings.

HIDE 'N' SEEK

Hide 'n' seek is a great way to introduce lots of social skills to your child but you can also create plenty of communication opportunities by making the game more complex and adding more rules and instructions for your child to follow. You can find more hide 'n' seek activities to play outside the house in Chapter 4.

Things to try

Hide 'n' seek in pairs

If your child is just learning how to play hide 'n' seek and you have enough people, you might like to try playing the game in pairs as that way you can pair up with your child and remind them what they have to do if they are hiding (e.g. find a good hiding spot, stay there and remember to be quiet until they are found), or seeking (e.g. look under things, open things, and remember to keep looking and listening for sounds that might indicate someone is hiding in a particular spot). If your child has difficulty identifying good hiding spots you might like to go around the house and garden with your child and identify what would be good spots to hide in. You might also like to put mats down in all the good hiding spots so that your child knows to find a mat and stay on it until someone finds them.

Toys/treasure hunt

Similar to a treasure hunt, you can play hide 'n' seek with your child's toys (or parts of a toy) all around the house or garden. This is a great way to teach your child to 'seek' all the toys and not get distracted (which sometimes happens when they are looking for other children!). You can encourage your child to count and find all the toys that were hidden and talk about where they might look to see where the toys are hidden. You can do the same with food for a picnic or a more traditional sweets/Easter egg hunt – your child will be a great seeker after that one!

Find by colours and other attributes

You can have lots of fun teaching your child colours while playing hide 'n' seek. For example, you could collect different items in the house that are a certain colour (e.g. 'red' items), and share the hiding and seeking of all the 'red' items all around the house and garden. If you are seeking the items you can 'pretend' to get it wrong sometimes to see if your child can pick you up on your mistakes. You can also extend this beyond colour and include attributes such as 'hard' items, 'furry' items or 'shiny' items, etc.

FUN WITH MATERIAL

Just a simple piece of material can provide hours of entertainment for a child with autism. You can get a range of different materials just by going to your local material shop and asking for remnants or off-cuts. All it takes is a little bit of creativity on your behalf and then you will find that there are lots of communication opportunities just waiting to occur, all without the need of expensive toys!

Things to try

Parachute

You can have lots of fun by turning a large piece of material (e.g. a bed sheet) into a pretend parachute. For example, you can create lots of communication opportunities by using two people to hold either end of the material and encouraging your child to choose to run under or jump over the material. Another idea is to place balloons, balls or soft toys on top of the parachute and make the items jump by lifting the parachute up and down.

Swinging and sliding

Your child might like to swing in a 'pretend' swing, which you can make by getting two people to hold a piece of material (2m x 1m), getting your child to sit/lie on it and lifting it and swinging it from side to side. You can easily change the swing to a slide by using just one adult and getting your child to sit on the piece of material while you pull your child around the room – like a sled! Lots of communication opportunities can be created with these games, such as getting your child to choose between 'swing' or 'slide', or make other requests such as 'big/little swing', 'fast/slow slide', counting how many swings they want!

Scarves

A simple bag of scarves can create lots of communication opportunities between you and your child. For example, by simply collecting a bag of scarves or small pieces of material (preferably see-through) you can create fun games by singing a song to the tune of 'drunken sailor' using the words,

'What shall we do with the scarves today?

What shall we do with the scarves today?

What shall we do with the scarves today?

What should we do first?

followed by ideas such as:

- *...put them on your face and blow.*

- *...put them on your eyes and say boo.*

- *...twirl them in the air and catch them.*

Tents and teepees

There is lots of fun to be had with your child by using large pieces of material (e.g. bed sheets, blankets, towels, etc.) and draping them over sofas, chairs or drying racks to make a tent-like space for you and your child to play under. You can play games in the tent, have picnics or bring in torches to play games such as torch chase (whereby you and your child have a torch and you have to catch each other's light with your own light).

Emergency/survival blanket

Emergency/survival blankets are giant pieces of shiny silver material (like a bed-sheet sized piece of aluminium foil) and are great fun to hide under with your child. Another fun idea is to use toys with lights and sounds underneath the blanket – because it is silver and crunchy this can create a fun disco-like environment (NB: Please remember to replace the emergency blanket if you have taken it out of a first aid kit!)

Roll like a hot dog

Some children with autism enjoy deep pressure or being rolled up in blankets with the tight feeling of the blanket around them. You can play a game with your child by getting them to lie down at the end of a long piece of material/yoga mat/rug, etc. and roll them up tightly in it (like a hot dog). You can squeeze them tight and then pretend to put cheese, pickles, salad and ketchup on either side of them, etc. You can create lots of communication opportunities around asking what pretend toppings they want on them... and then eat them up!

Warning! Be aware of the risk of suffocation when wrapping a child in a blanket.

Things to remember

If you are using the material with lots of different children, for hygiene reasons it is important to wash it regularly.

FUN WITH LYCRA

Lycra is a special type of material that is extremely stretchy and many children with autism seem to like all the different activities you can do with this type of material. Lots of communication opportunities can be created by all the different actions you can perform with this material – for example, you can teach your child to request: 'wrapping', 'rolling', 'pulling', 'stretching' and lots more!

Warning! Be aware of the risk of suffocation when wrapping children in fabric.

Things to try

The Lycra stretch

You can have lots of fun with Lycra by stretching it over your child. For example, if you get a piece of Lycra about 2m x 1m you can use it like a parachute but instead of hoving it over your child's head you can stretch it tightly around your child, or hold it down low while your child stands up in it, pushing and stretching the material in all kinds of different ways. It's a good idea to take photos and show your child what it looks like when they try to push through the Lycra.

Lycra pull

Lots of fun and communication opportunities can be created by pulling pieces of Lycra with your child. For example, you might like to hold one edge of the

Lycra while your child holds the other end, and then you might count or say 'Ready, Steady, Go!' and then pull as hard as you can on the material (you can either step backwards to pull or lean backwards until you fall!). You can also create more communication by talking with your child about letting the material go and watching it fly upwards!

Lycra tent

You can have lots of fun by sitting on the floor with your child and pulling Lycra tightly over you and your child like a tent, sitting on it to hold it in place. You can play lots of games under the Lycra tent, have a picnic, tell stories or pretend you are hiding from someone!

Lycra sled

Lycra is great for turning into a pretend sled and is fun for your child to lie on while you pull them around on the floor! Lots of communication opportunities can be created with this game, such as getting your child to request 'fast/slow slide', or counting how long they can stay on the sled before falling off (by making quick turns with the Lycra you can make it harder for your child to stay on).

Lycra 'stretchy' swing

By getting your child to lie down on a large piece of Lycra and having two adults hold either end you can have lots of fun making a stretchy swing, whereby you can lift your child up in the material, swing them or bounce them up and down. This can produce lots of communication about bigger swings or bouncier swings, and you might also like to roll them up tightly in the Lycra before swinging!

Lycra trampoline

You can have lots of fun with your child by turning a large piece of Lycra into a pretend trampoline. For example, by getting your child to hold one end of the Lycra with their arms spread out wide and you holding the other end, you can place your child's favourite toys, teddies, soft balls or balloons onto the top of the material and flick the Lycra up and down so all the items jump up!

Giant sock

Some children with autism really like a feeling of pressure and tightness around them. By sewing a large piece of Lycra into a long thin bag with a hole big enough to climb in and out of, your child might like to use it as a giant body sock to crawl into when they need to get away for a while, or they might like to crawl into it, stretch out against it and make funny statues (it's good to take photographs of this one), or it can be used as a swing with two adults holding and swinging it with your child's head poking out one end.

PARTY GAMES

Party games are a great way to get your child interacting with other children because the games are always a lot of fun for everyone involved. It's a good idea to practise these games with your child before expecting them to be able to enjoy them with other children – particularly when they might later be in a party situation where there is often a lot of chaos involved.

Things to try

Dressing up game

You can have a lot of fun with a dressing up game that is very similar to Pass the Parcel but with clothes! First, you will need to fill a large bag or basket with dressing up clothes, old hats, scarves, odd socks, boots, etc. (and if possible include some joke items such as fake ears and plastic spectacles). Then, you sit in a circle on the floor with family members or other children with music playing, passing the bag/basket around the circle. When the music stops whoever is holding the bag needs to reach in and pull out one article of clothing (without looking) and put it on. This is a great game with lots of communication opportunities for sharing, turn-taking and commenting. You might also like to have a hand-held mirror close by so your child can look at themselves, and a camera is also a good idea so you can talk about how silly you looked after the game has finished.

Balloon pop

If your child is not scared of the noise that balloons make when they pop then this game could be a lot of fun. You will need to spend some time setting up the game; if your child is not too excited you might be able to include them in the setting-up process.

1. Start by getting a few small prizes (have the same number as the number of people playing the game) to give out at the end of the game.

2. You will then need to write the name of the prizes on small pieces of paper (or draw simple pictures of the items).

3. You will then need to roll and push the small pieces of paper into separate balloons, inflate the balloons and tie them off: now the game is ready to start.

4. Line the children/adults up on one side of the room and the balloons on the other side.

5. Then, when you signal, the children have to run across to the other side, pop one balloon each (without using teeth or sharp objects) and then pick up the piece of paper and take it to you.

6. They then receive their prize.

This provides lots of communication opportunities, such as following directions when setting the game up and also following social rule games like lining up, waiting for 'go', and only popping one balloon.

Pass it along

Similar to the game Pass the Parcel, this game has a 'prize' or an item in every layer of paper. This game is great for providing opportunities to teach children how to comment and also how to wait for something exciting (the item). You can also put items in that relate to a story (e.g. pieces of pretend food that relate to the Hungry Caterpillar) or parts of a toy that you make up as each piece is unravelled (e.g. Mr Potato Head).

Memory game

You can have lots of fun by playing memory games in a social way. For example, you might like to place some favourite toys (or even just household items) on a tray. Show the children the items and encourage them to try to remember as many as they can. Then cover the items with a cloth and see if the children can remember what the items were. If this is too easy, you can make the children wait a few minutes before they tell you what they have remembered, or increase the number of items that you are asking them to remember. If they are having trouble remembering what the items are you might let them put their hand under the cloth and see if feeling the item helps them remember.

Feather race

This is a fun and quick game that can be played almost anywhere and can create lots of communication opportunities. By giving your children and their familes a feather (coloured ones are great as are ones that look a little different, with a coloured mark on them etc.) they can be used to blow across the table. For example, line the feathers up on a table and get the children to stand behind the feather, and when you give them a sign to start the race, encourage the children to keep blowing their feathers until they fall off the end of the table (or a finishing line that you have drawn). You can also do the same by getting your children to blow through straws, or you might like to use ping-pong balls instead of feathers.

Musical chairs

This game is great for creating communication opportunities around following instructions, social skills and waiting. There are two main ways you can play this game. For both versions of the game you will need to arrange some chairs (the same number of chairs as there are children) in the centre of the room in a circle but with the seats facing outwards. Then, you will need to put some music on and while the music is playing you need to encourage your children to walk/hop/skip, etc. around the chairs in a circle. When the music stops the children need to rush and sit down on a chair. One version of this game is that each time you play the music you take one chair away and the child left standing has to sit out of the game, with the last person to sit on the one chair at the end being the winner. Or, each turn you take a chair away but instead of the children sitting out they just have to sit on top of each other on the chairs that are left!

The Chocolate Game (with a fork and knife)

The Chocolate Game, described earlier in Chapter 1, is a great family or party game to play. You will need a block of chocolate (but don't break it up), a tray, a knife, a fork, a dice and a timer. The idea of the game is that you sit in a circle on the floor or around the table and you take it in turns rolling the dice. When you roll a six you have one minute (or longer if you think that necessary) on the timer, to try to cut one piece of chocolate with a knife and fork! If this is too hard for your child you might need to change the rules a little or help them out. This only really works if your child likes chocolate (you can always change the foods so long as you make whatever it is hard to get!).

'I SPY'

'I spy' is a great game that can create lots of different opportunities for communication and social skills development. For example, 'I spy' can help your child to learn to look at the same thing as you (i.e. joint attention) or learn about asking/answering questions. You might also like to use this game to create opportunities for your child to practise new language skills, such as sounds/letters or concepts such as colours or other descriptive words.

Things to try

Letters and sounds

Traditionally 'I spy' is played by looking around the room and asking/answering questions such as 'I spy, with my little eye, something that starts with the letter "k"'. This game can be played anywhere in the house, in the car or on the bus and can be a great way of engaging your child to interact with you and learn to answer and ask questions. If your child is just learning their sounds or letters you can make this game a little easier by putting blank stickers on items around the room and writing on the stickers with your child the letter that corresponds to the first letter/sound of that word, for example, sticking a sticker with the letter 'w' on the window. The same types of games and strategies can be used if your child is learning phonics or the sounds of letters.

Colours and shapes

You can create lots of opportunities for helping your child learn and use the names of colours by changing the 'I spy' game to focus on coloured items. For example, you could say 'I spy, with my little eye, something that is red,' and encourage your child to look around the room for red items and guess what you might be spying. You can modify this game if your child is having difficulty (particularly when items have multiple colours) by placing coloured stickers on different items and then you could say 'I spy, with my little eye, something that has a green sticker on it.' You can also play the same game but focusing on shapes, and when your child has mastered that you can combine the two (colours and shape).

Torches

You can also play 'I spy' in the dark simply by getting a torch and shining it on an item (just quickly flash the item with the torch) that you want your child to 'spy'. You might also like to try this at storytime and flash the torch on certain characters or items in the book.

Magic stickers

When your child is learning to play 'I spy' you might initially need to help them by using visual supports. For example, you might need to go around the room and identify things that you might 'spy' by placing reusable stickers/post-it notes and labelling them, so these act as a prompt for when they choose to spy an item.

SINGING

Singing is great way to engage your child at all communication levels, for example, your child might simply like listening to you sing, join in with actions of a song, finish the end of the song or choose different songs for you to sing.

Things to try

Song-choice boards

Song-choice boards are made up of small drawings or pictures on a piece of paper or board to illustrate songs, e.g. draw a star for 'Twinkle Twinkle Little Star' or a bus for 'The Wheels on the Bus', and are a great way of reminding your children what song choices are available to them. If your child is learning to communicate but can't yet say all the names of the songs, you can encourage your child to point at the picture of the song that they want to hear.

Action songs

There are many fun children's songs that encourage the use of actions. These songs are great for encouraging early communication skills such as imitation and anticipation. For example, you might like to sing a familiar song and either 'forget' what to do or do the wrong actions in order to provoke a response and interaction from your child. You can also have a lot of fun by changing the speed of the song and actions, either by being silly and going too fast or by slowing it down to help your child learn the actions.

Microphones

Toy, real or pretend microphones are great fun when singing with your child. You can encourage your child to request different ways they want you to sing into the microphone (e.g. funny voice singing, whisper singing, squeaky singing, loud singing). You might also like to use the microphone in a turn-taking game, where each person sings a line from the song and passes the microphone along to the next person. You can have lots of fun with this game by changing how slowly or quickly you sing each line.

Guess the song

Your child probably knows many songs just by hearing one or two lines. These songs might be jingles from television advertisements, nursery rhymes, pop songs or theme songs from their favourite television show or movies. You can create a guessing game by simply singing one or two lines of the song and asking your child what the song is from or to sing the rest of the song. If you don't want to sing the song you may be able to find video or audio recordings on the internet.

TICKLES AND GIGGLES

Tickling games are a great way for your child to learn to enjoy early social interaction with others. Tickles can provide lots of opportunities for requesting things likes 'more' and 'stop', or encouraging your child to tell you where they want to be tickled (e.g. tummy, foot, head, etc.).

Things to try

Tickles all round

You can turn tickles into a fun game simply by getting your child to request where they want the tickles on the body (or, vice versa, you can tell your child where you want to be tickled). You might like to use a visual choice board if your child is still learning the names of all the body parts. You can also turn this game into a song where you sing...

Round and round the garden
Like a teddy bear
One step, two step
Tickles…where?

Tickle bag

Fingers are great for tickling and so are feathers, but have you ever thought to try back scratchers, brushes, loofahs, cellophane or Koosh balls? To extend communication and requesting you might like to try putting a tickle bag together containing lots of items that you can tickle your child with. Before you know it your child will be asking 'I want toothbrush tickle on my toes.'

Tickle and chomp

You can play another tickle game by pretending to eat different parts of your child's body. For example, in a loud voice you could say, 'I'm going to eat your... (wait for your child to get excited)... toes!' and then take your child's foot towards your mouth, pretend to eat it (with loud chomping noises) and then tickle their feet. This game is great for building anticipation and eye contact, and in no time at all your child will be telling you what part of the body they want you to eat.

Smelly feet

Smelly feet is a great game to get your child to giggle and ask for more. The idea of this game is you grab your child's foot and pretend that it is really smelly by making 'Pooey' comments. You can build anticipation and suspense into this game by gradually getting your nose closer to your child's foot and becoming more dramatic about how much it smells! Or, if your child is wearing shoes and socks, you can gradually peel each layer off, and when you get to the bare foot you can pretend to pass out on the floor because it smells so much! This game is great for getting your child to giggle but also for the pleasure of sharing a joke and being silly.

Blowing 'raspberries'

Blowing 'raspberries' on your child's tummy or various body parts is sure to get both you and your child giggling. For those who haven't experienced this joy, blowing a 'raspberry' involves you making a rude noise by putting your tongue between your lips and blowing and then pressing your vibrating lips onto different parts of your child's body (most commonly done on the tummy, hands, arms and face).

Elevator up

If your child is little and you can pick them up easily, you might like to try playing a game called 'Elevator up'. This game involves holding your child around the waist, and lifting them up and down like an elevator. To start the game off, you might like to hold your child and say the word 'up' as you lift them up bit by bit. After your child is familiar with the game, you can pause between each lift and wait for them to smile, giggle or request 'up/down' (through speech or pointing) before lifting them.

Magic buttons

By simply drawing a few circles on some paper and pretending they are 'magic buttons' with special features you can create lots of fun for both you and your child. This game is played by pretending each button has a special feature such as an action (e.g. tickles, jumping, chasing, sleeping) or noise (e.g. car horns and sirens, animals, etc.). When your child presses the 'magic button' you act out the different features.

MOTIVATE ME WITH OUTSIDE GAMES

Many children with autism enjoy being active and by being outside with your child you have an even bigger space which, in turn, means you can go bigger, messier and noisier than ever! Being outside doesn't just have to be in a back garden – your child might also like to play games in different playgrounds, sports grounds or parks.

Often outside games involve other children and adults and are therefore a great way to practise social skills. If you are at a park you might also like to ask other children to join in your games. For example, if you are blowing giant bubbles in a park, other children in the park might show interest. You could support your child in learning how to ask a friend to join them in their game, and it is also a great way for your child to learn skills such as waiting and turn-taking.

Being outside also offers opportunities for your child to run around and be more energetic and active. It is sometimes a good idea to allocate regular 'outside' games to help break up work or games that require lots of sitting and concentrating time (e.g. school work or inside games).

Also, by playing games outside you can be a little more adventurous and creative without having to worry about cleaning the mess up afterwards. For example, if your child likes bubbles you might like to try giant bubble wands with lots of bubble mixture. Or if it is a hot day you might like to play catch and throw with water-filled balloons, or other games that involve things that are messy such as sand or mud, etc.

GARDEN GAMES

Gardens are a great way to motivate your child to communicate because you can use the things in the garden to play with, use the extra space to move around, or take toys from inside and play with them in the sunshine!

Things to try

Giant bubble wands

Bubbles in the garden are a great way to encourage lots of different communication skills. For example, you can ask your child if they want to blow the bubble themselves, hold the wand up in into the wind, or just run around with the wand to make the bubbles. Another game that you might like to play is bubble fighting, whereby you each have a wand and you attack each other by blowing bubbles onto each other (like paint balling).

Streamers

By tying long thin strips of material, ribbon or streamers to a stick you can swirl them around in the wind to make patterns. You might like to try playing chase with the streamers by trying to jump on each other's ribbon ends. You can teach lots of language concepts with this game, such as 'twirl', 'twist', 'jump', 'chase' and 'high/low'.

Obstacle courses

By using old tyres, hoops, rope, cones, wooden planks, chalk, play tunnels, or mini trampolines you can make fun obstacle courses for you and your child to get moving. You might like to play some music during the obstacle course and play a 'stop and go' game to the music (e.g. when the music is playing you can run, but when the music stops so do you).

Chalk and water painting

By giving your child a paintbrush and a pot of water or some chalk you can have fun by drawing or painting on walls, fences, or concrete (where this is permissible). Lots of communication opportunities can be created by getting your child to ask you to draw different shapes or pictures or by describing what they have drawn. You can also draw shapes/write numbers and play jumping games on the pictures (e.g. hopscotch, follow the numbers).

Mud pies

By mixing different amounts of dirt and water together you can make a range of consistencies of mud. You can encourage your child to explore the mud by putting their hands or feet in it or picking it up and throwing it at the fence or a tree. You can use plant pots and sticks to create sculptures (e.g. like sand castles). Lots of fun words can be taught with these games such as 'Oh, yuck!', 'Splat', 'It feels squishy.'

Watering the plants

By filling up water bottles and spray bottles you can have lots of fun watering the plants. You can create lots of communication opportunities around language concepts such as spraying the water 'high' and 'low'. Or you might like to try filling up buckets and pouring them on the ground to make pretend rivers or puddles to jump in.

Hide 'n' seek

If your child is just learning how to play hide 'n' seek and if you have enough people, you might like to try playing the game in pairs – that way you can pair up with your child and remind them what they have to do if they are hiding (e.g. find a good hiding spot, stay there and remember to be quiet until they are found), or seeking (e.g. look under things, open things, and remember to keep looking and listening for sounds that might indicate someone is hiding in a particular spot). If your child has difficulty identifying good hiding spots you might like to go around the house and garden with your child identifying what would be good spots to hide in. You might also like to put coloured cones down in all the good hiding spots so that your child knows where to hide or stay near until someone finds them.

Treasure hunt

Food treats, party toys (e.g. balloons, sparklers, etc.) or your child's favourite toys (e.g. small dinosaurs, toy cars, marbles, etc.) hidden around the garden or park are great motivating ways to get your child moving. You might need to give your child a small bag/bucket to help carry the treasures as they find them. Once the bag/bucket is full you can encourage your child to tip it all out and count or show, name and/or describe what treasures they have found.

WATER PLAY/SWIMMING

Playing with water can be lots of fun on a hot summer's day! Many children with autism really enjoy playing with water either at bath time or when swimming, in the sink or in the special water trays that you often find in schools. You can create many communication opportunities with your child just by playing with the water by itself or by adding toys to the fun!

Things to try

Duck, dive and find

You can create lots of fun games by putting items that sink (e.g. keys, coins or weighted rings, etc.) into a pool, the bath, sink or bucket. You can then encourage your child to duck under the water or reach with their arm into the water and try to collect all the items that have sunk to the bottom. You can also create communication opportunities around counting the items and getting them to show/talk about the items that they have found.

Water aerobics

Water aerobics is a great game to play with your child to help burn off some of that extra energy that they might have. It is also great for your child to learn how to follow instructions (e.g. stepping side to side while clapping, etc.). You can also play 'Simon Says' in the water.

Songs and actions

Singing simple songs with actions in the water can be lots of fun for you and your child. For example, songs like 'Ring a Ring a Rosie' are great because the last action is falling down, which means you can put your head under the water. Other songs that can be fun include 'Row, Row your Boat' and the 'Hokey Cokey' because the actions take a lot more effort in the water. You can create lots of communication opportunities by singing and pausing at crucial lines to encourage initiation.

Holding your breath

You can play simple games in the pool like holding your breath under water, but this game is best played when you both go under the water together and see who can stay under the longest. You can create lots of communication opportunities by saying 'Ready, Steady, Go!' before going under. You can also have some really nice eye contact under the water with each other, and you can also encourage your child to count (or watch you count) with your fingers while under the water. You and your child might like to wear goggles so you can see each other clearly.

Warning! Please monitor your child carefully during this activity as it does not take long for a child to drown.

Beach ball

You can also play lots of games with your child without having to even get in the water! For example, you might have a soft rubber ball or a beach ball that you can throw to your child from the poolside. This game is great for encouraging your child to request where they want the ball to be thrown (e.g. 'up high', 'in front', or 'to the left/right', etc.). Depending on your child's communication abilities this might be done verbally or simply by pointing to where they want the ball to go.

Noodle tag

'Pool noodles' are those giant foam/polystyrene tubes that can help children learn to float in the pool but they are also great to play lots of different games with. One particular game you might like to play is noodle tag. This game involves one person with the noodle chasing and tagging their friends in the pool. This game is great for turn-taking and generally learning social skills that come with playing games with other children.

Spray bottles

Spray bottles are inexpensive and you can have lots of fun and create endless communication opportunities with your child with them in a pool, the bath or just outside! For example, you could spray each other, use them to spray and knock over plastic bottles on the side of the pool, see whose spray can go the highest/furthest, or who can empty their bottle the first by spraying. If you are spraying in the bath or sink you could add colour dye to the water and create fun patterns as the coloured water mixes!

Ping-pong pop

Ping-pong balls are so much fun in the pool, the bath or just a tub of water! You can create lots of fun games with them by helping your child hold them under the water, releasing them and watching them 'pop' out of the water. You can also play blowing games by placing the ping-pong balls on top of the water and racing to see who can blow them with their mouth across the water the quickest.

Cork grab

Cork grab is a great game to play in the bath or a pool. By simply placing all the corks that you have (or other floating items such as ping-pong balls) in the water you can make a game out of it by racing to grab all the corks and then comparing with each other at the end to see how many corks each person was able to grab!

Pool chase

Playing chase in the pool is fun but hard work! The water really slows you down but also helps get rid of any extra energy that your child might have. You can create lots of opportunities for communication and social/play skill development by introducing a little bit of structure into this game. For example, when playing chase in the pool you might introduce a rule that the person who is chasing needs to stand in the corner of the pool and count to ten before chasing the other person, to give them time to get a head start.

Colours and glitter

You can have lots of fun with your child by adding food dye and/or glitter to a tub of water. You can create lots of patterns and swirls and provide lots of opportunities for your child to make requests and comment about what the water looks like.

Wet sponge throw

By dipping a sponge into water and playing catch with your child you can have lots of fun in the park or garden on a hot summer's day because each time you catch the sponge you inevitably get very wet! All you need for this game is two buckets of water (one for each of you) and one wet sponge. This game is great for teaching your child to be silly and learning to enjoy watching their friends get wet!

HIDE 'N' SEEK

As mentioned in Chapter 3, hide 'n' seek is a great social game that is fun for playing both indoors and outdoors. All you need is a little creativity and a smile on your face, and before you know it you will have your child giggling and learning about all the fun that they can have when playing with other children or adults.

Things to try

Back garden

As mentioned earlier in this chapter under 'Garden Games', if your child is just learning how to play hide 'n' seek and you have enough people, you might like to try playing the game in pairs as that way you can pair up with your child and remind them what they have to do if they are hiding (e.g. find a good hiding spot, stay there and remember to be quiet until they are found), or seeking (e.g. look under things, open things, and remember to keep looking and listening for sounds that might indicate someone is hiding in a particular spot). If your child has difficulty identifying good hiding spots you might like to go around the house and garden with them identifying what would be good spots to hide in. You might also like to put coloured cones down in all the good hiding spots so that your child knows where to hide until someone finds them.

Treasure hunt

You can set up a treasure hunt in the garden or park with your child's favourite toys (e.g. farm animals). You can teach your child to follow lots of instructions by asking them to close their eyes while you hide them all around the garden. Your child will have lots of fun as they run around, find them all and put them in a bucket (you might tell your child that you have hidden a certain number of toys/items so they can count them to see if they have found them all). Or you can get your child to guess where you might have hidden them by verbally asking 'Is there a toy under the slide?' or by pointing to various things in the park and your child looking under or behind them to see if there is a toy. This is good for teaching the 'yes/no' response.

Paper trail

If your child is able to read, or understand verbal instructions (when you read them aloud) they might really like playing a paper trail game in the garden or at the park. A paper trail game involves you writing some instructions down on little pieces of paper and hiding them all over the garden/park. The idea of the game is that your child has to find each piece of paper, which has a clue on it about where the next piece of paper is, which eventually leads to a prize at the end.

Things to remember

Some parks and sports grounds are very large and probably fairly easy for your child to wander off in or, worse, get lost in. If your child can understand, it might be a good idea to explain to them before you play some of these games about how far they are allowed to go across the park. You might like to point to specific boundaries (certain trees or play equipment) and ask them not to go beyond those points. Or, you might like to walk around the boundaries with your child so they can see the boundaries and experience where they are not supposed to go beyond. Another idea is if you have a very long piece of rope or string you can lay it on the ground all around the boundary (like a cricket ground) to provide a visual marker for your child.

PLAYGROUND TOYS AND EQUIPMENT

There are often lots of things to play with and lots of equipment available in schools, however, sometimes we need to help our children learn to have fun with playground equipment in different ways.

Things to try

Skipping rope

There are lots of skipping games you might like to teach your child to play and enjoy. You can teach these in the traditional way of skipping while also introducing jumping songs, or counting or saying the letters of the alphabet each time they jump. You could also wiggle the skipping rope on the ground and pretend it is a poisonous snake that your child has to jump over and run away from.

Elastic/french skipping

There are lots of different games you can play with elastics (a three to four metre piece of elastic rope) and they are all great for teaching your child social skills, learning to sing songs and imitating language concepts such as prepositions ('in', 'on', 'out', etc.). If you search online for elastic games you will find lots of different action songs that you might like to try with your child. For example, you might find a song like

'In, Out, Side by Side'. This game involves two people to hold the elastic around their ankles while the third person jumps in and out of the elastic, following these chanted directions:

In	(jump into the middle)
Out	(jump out – one foot on each side)
Side	(jump one foot in middle, one foot on one side)
By Side	(jump one foot in middle, one foot on the other side)
On	(jump on the elastic, one foot on each side)
In	(jump into the middle)
Out	(jump out – one foot on each side).

If the sequence is done correctly then raise the elastic to mid-calf and so on.

Ball in a bucket

There are often lots of balls lying around in a school playground, particularly tennis balls. If you can find a bucket you could play a game with your child by getting one of you to hold the bucket while the other one has to try to throw the balls into the bucket. You can make this more difficult by moving the bucket around. There are lots of communication opportunities you can create with this game, such as counting the balls, and getting your child to tell you where to move with the bucket (e.g. 'up high', 'down low', 'closer', etc.). You could also play a similar game with mini-bean bags or rubber quoits.

Obstacle course

There is often lots of playground equipment lying around in schools, which would be perfect for making an obstacle course. By using tyres, hoops, rope, cones, wooden planks, chalk, play tunnels, swing and slides, you can take it in turns with your child to make different obstacle courses – this is great for making up and following instructions. You might like to play some music while moving through the obstacle course and play a 'stop and go' game to the music (e.g. when the music is playing you can run, but when the music stops so do you).

Chalk trail

There is often chalk lying around in school playgrounds and this can be great for creating chalk trails. For example, by simply drawing a long line all around the playground with chalk you can play chase games with your child where you have to stay on the lines. Or you might like to write numbers all over the playground whereby you and your child have to race to find all the chalk numbers and run to them in order!

Washing-line tennis!

If you just get a little bit creative with some of the playground toys you can create so many different games. For example, if your child likes to hit balls with a tennis racket, cricket bat, baseball bat, etc., you might like to try putting a tennis ball in an old stocking or sock and tying it to a tree or line. Your child can play by themselves, or if you have two bats you can take turns in hitting the ball to each other (just watch out you don't hit each other with the racquets).

Big physio(therapy) balls

Giant physiotherapy balls are great to play with outside. You can play games like giant 'catch' with your child. You can leapfrog over the giant ball by rolling it through your legs to each other. You might like to use it to play a game of giant skittles (e.g. knocking over plastic bottles filled with water). Your child might also like to lie down on a mat while you roll the ball over them, pretending that the ball is a giant rolling pin and that they are the cookie/pizza dough and you are going to roll them out (great for children that like deep pressure).

SAND AND SNOW PLAY

When you play with sand and snow outside you can really go to town and have some fun with your child without having to worry about cleaning him or her afterwards! Sand and snow are favourites with most children, but children with autism often particularly enjoy the sensory experience of holding, pouring or patting the sand and snow.

Things to try

Castles

Building sand, snow, or even dirt castles is a favourite of many children. You can create lots of communication opportunities around all the actions required to build and knock down the castles. For example, you might encourage your child to use words or actions that represent 'scoop', 'fill', 'pat', 'turn it over' or 'crash'. You might also like to include counting while building or knocking down the castle – for example, you might count the number of scoops to fill the bucket or you might count down before knocking down or jumping onto the castle.

Writing and pictures

If you rake over a tray of sand or smooth out some snow you can have lots of fun by using it to write or draw different things in. You might like to write secret messages in the sand or draw a part of a picture and get your child to guess what the picture might be.

Instant snow

If you don't live in a place where you get much snow, don't worry as you can always make your own with a product called 'instant snow' (just search the internet for 'instant snow' to find out where you can buy it). Lots of fun and communication opportunities can also be created by making the instant snow. For example, you can get your child to count out how many teaspoons of instant snow powder to put into the bowl, then you can talk about how much water to add and ask your child to stir slowly or quickly depending on how fast you pour the water. After you have made the snow you can hide things in it, squeeze it, mould it or throw it at each other (best done outside, though!).

Hide 'n' seek in the sand

Playing hide 'n' seek in a sand box is great for children with autism who like the sensation of raking their hands through the sand. You can turn this into a game by hiding their favourite toys, magnetic letters, etc. in the sand and getting your child to find them. You can make this more exciting or difficult by using a timer and only giving them a certain amount of time to find all the items. You might also like to use a blindfold or turn the activity into a competition if you have more than one child finding the items (i.e. count the items at the end to see who found the most items).

Sand toys and tools

There are a lot of toys and tools that you can buy specifically for playing in the sand, or you can just use containers from the kitchen, etc. Many children with autism like pouring sand from up high or from cup to cup. Sand wheels, where you can pour sand in the top and watch it turn the wheel, are lots of fun, particularly for children who enjoying toys that spin. You can create lots of communication opportunities with these games by getting your child to request what toy or tools they want, or you can count how many times they can pour the sand from cup to cup before the sand all falls out.

Sloppy sand!

Sand comes in all different textures – some sand is fine and some sand is coarse and if you add water, it can become very sloppy. By mixing different amounts of water with the sand you can create lots of textures for your child to play with. For example, you can mould firm wet sand into different shapes or if you add more water to it you can squeeze it through your fingers or push it through small holes and make sand worms!

Magic Sand, Space Sand or Mars Sand

There are some fun sand products on the market with names such as 'Magic Sand'. This special sand changes texture in warm water and is great for creating layered patterns; its texture is so versatile that you can sculpt and create things like bridges, walls and towers.

Sand and snow angels

Those who live in colder climates where the snow falls regularly are probably familiar with making 'snow angels' with your children. But, guess what, you can actually make them in the sand too! Your children will love doing this, and it is great for learning how to follow instructions. For example, you can make sand/snow angels by getting your child to lie down flat in the sand/snow, then getting them to brush their arms between their head and waist in a sweeping motion. Then ask them to move their legs apart as far as they will go (like doing a jumping jack while lying on your back!). Then get your child to carefully stand up and look at the angel indent they have made in the snow/sand.

Coloured snow

You can create lots of fun with your child by bringing a pile of snow in from outside and dripping food colouring into it to see where this flows and what colours it makes. Your child can request what colours they want and comment about what colour it turns when you put lots of different colours together.

MESSY PLAY (NON-FOOD ITEMS)

Often when we think of messy play we think of using lots of food items, but that doesn't always have to be the case! There are lots of different things under your kitchen sink, in your bathroom, in your laundry and in your craft box that are also great for using in messy play. However, you will need to be careful because many of these things might be toxic. Before you start, make sure your child knows this type of messy play is not for eating!

Things to try

Gloop and slime

You can often buy gloop and slime from magic/toy stores but you never really get that much to play with. Not only is it easy to make, you can also have lots of fun making it with your child and that way you will have more than enough to go around. Gloop is great fun to play with because it has such a funny feeling when you play with it. You can encourage your child to try to grab it, squeeze it through their hands, dribble it from one container to another (colanders and sieves are great fun too) – all of which provides lots of fun and lots of communication opportunities!

All you need is:

- 1 teaspoon of borax[1]

- ⅓ cup water

---

1   Also known as sodium borate/sodium tetraborate, or disodium tetraborate

- ½ cup PVA glue

- ½ cup water

- food colouring.

Mix the borax and the ⅓ cup water in one jug and put aside. Then mix the PVA, ½ cup water and food colour together. Add the two mixtures together, and your gloop is ready when it no longer sticks to the spoon!

Soap flakes

Soap flakes (e.g. Lux) are great fun to play with when you just add a little bit of water to them because they make a great slimy goo texture. You can add food colouring to change the colour of the goo and mould it into different shapes, or you can add more water to make it thinner and then blow into it through straws to make really big bubbles in it.

Sawdust

You can have a lot of fun with your child by simply mixing PVA glue and sawdust (you can often get sawdust from pet stores) together and sculpting it into different shapes and forms (e.g. animals, faces). You can then leave them to dry and they will harden but still remain a little bit bendy. You might like to make characters from a book or make your own family, etc.

Be careful when you use sawdust because it is easy to get it into your eyes, or if your child has asthma the sawdust might aggravate it.

Shaving cream/foam

If you spread a thin layer of shaving cream or foam in a tray or on a tabletop you can encourage your child to use their finger or a paintbrush to draw or write in it (your child might prefer to wear gloves if they don't like getting their hands dirty). You can keep drawing over and over again by simply smoothing the cream/foam back over. You can also use foods such as custard or yoghurt and you get the same effect (but watch out as it can get messy).

Shredded paper

You can have lots of fun by playing hide 'n' seek in a box full of shredded paper. You can take turns in hiding items (e.g. animals, coins, food) in the box and reaching in and trying to find them. You could either time how long it takes each of you to find all the items or you could both put your hands in at the same time and see who can get the most (you will probably keep grabbing each other's hands!).

MOTIVATE ME AT
HOME AND SCHOOL

There are lots of things both at home or at school that your child will like. You probably don't need to buy new things but just need to start thinking about how you might use these toys in a different way to help motivate your child. It is a bit of an art to coming up with lots of different ideas but once you get the hang of it your child will be having fun, learning and communicating before you know it. Recycling toys is a great way to help maintain motivation in the home and school. Try not to leave all your toys out for your child to play with all the time – hide some away and rotate the use of them.

RAMPS, RUNS AND ROLLING TOYS

Lots of children with autism like things that go down ramps and runs, such as car ramps and marble runs and toys that roll down things (like balls rolling down guttering). If your child likes these things it is important to start thinking what things you have around the home that you could use to get the same action as that way you can create lots of communication opportunities as well as have lots of fun!

Things to try

Pounding balls

If you go into a toy store there will generally be a toy available that involves a hammer (or you can use your hand) that hits balls through a hole, that then roll down a ramp (sometimes called 'pound-a-ball'). This is a great toy for teaching turn-taking, or you can intentionally add balls that are too big for the toy and encourage your child to choose the ball that fits with the toy. The balls are also usually different colours so you can create communication opportunities for your child by getting them to ask for a specific colour ball or state how many balls they want.

Marble runs

Marble runs are a great toy for teaching almost any communication skill, and children with autism (as well as adults) seem to really get a lot of pleasure out of this toy. For those who are not familiar with them, a marble run is a toy that has lots of little ramps/gutter pieces that you put on top of each other and then put marbles down them and watch them roll down and change direction through all the ramps. This provides lots of communication opportunities because there are so many choices and the pieces come in all different sizes and colours. You can also talk about the number of pieces or marbles, and your child will most likely need to learn to request help, particularly around building the run. You can build your own marble run or you can get your child to follow visual instructions to build more complex marble runs.

Roof guttering

An offcut of roof guttering is great for turning into a ramp for rolling cars down, or marbles, ping-pong balls and lots more. There are lots of choices for your child to make about what they want to roll down. You might also like to race different things down the guttering and talk to your child about what came first, second, third, last, etc. You might also like to roll different items down together and as they scatter around on the floor you can race to find them and pick them all up.

Bath fun!

Baths often have a nice curved part to them at the end which is great for lining up and rolling rubber/plastic balls down. It can be even more fun when there is a little bit of water in the bath as the balls become very slippery to hold onto. This creates lots of communication opportunities around turn-taking, catching, rolling and seeing how many you can hold on to at one end at the same time before they all start rolling down into the bath!

Slides

Slides are great to roll things down. Lots of fun can be had with rolling your child's favourite toys and teddy bears down. Your child might also like to slide down the slide and see if they beat their toys in reaching the end.

MR POTATO HEAD

Mr Potato Head is one of those toys that you can teach almost any communication skill with! It is made by Hasbro and can be found in nearly every toy store, or sometimes if you are lucky you can find a whole lot of Mr Potato Heads for sale on eBay. There are lots of different sizes and versions of Mr Potato Head and there is probably one that will really appeal to your particular child. For example, there is a Mr Potato Head that dresses up as farm animals, famous basketball, football and baseball teams, characters from the latest movies like 'Star Wars', 'Indiana Jones', 'Spider Man' – the list goes on and on.

Things to try

Build the potato

You can create lots of communication opportunities simply by building Mr Potato Head. For example, you might put all of Mr Potato Head's parts into a container and hold on to it to keep control of the activity. It is a good idea if your child is unfamiliar with the game to introduce what you are going to call all the different parts. Then, piece by piece, your child can request different parts to make up Mr Potato Head. If your child is unable to verbally request you might simply hold up two pieces and they have to point to the piece that they want.

Mr Silly

There is not only one way to build Mr Potato Head – you can be really silly and teach your child about how to make jokes with him. For example, you might put his arm on the top of his head or put his eyes where his arms go. You can create lots of communication opportunities around asking questions like 'Is that normal or is that silly?', and this is a good way to introduce humour with your child!

Different sizes

Mr Potato Head comes in all different sizes and if you have different-sized pieces you can teach concepts like 'big/little', or make comments such as 'too big' or 'too little'. You might also try to teach your child to answer with a 'yes/no' response. For example, you might give your child a piece of Mr Potato Head and ask 'Does it fit?' and encourage your child to answer 'Yes' or 'No'.

Barrier games

If you have lots of parts to Mr Potato Head that are the same you can play a game whereby you have to try to build the same Mr Potato Head as your child. For example, similar to the game 'Battleships', you pick out all the pieces that you have two of, and place one in each of two containers. You then sit opposite your child with a barrier in the middle (it could be a book propped up, etc.) and a container of pieces on each side. You then give instructions to each other to see if you can make identical Mr Potato Heads. For example, you might say to your child 'Put the blue shoes on' while you put the blue shoes on your Mr Potato Head and your child, we hope, follows your directions on the other side of the barrier. You can then remove the barrier to see if your potatoes match. If your child is having trouble with this game it might help to play in pairs. Your child can then tell you what to do – 'Put the red nose on' – while they do the same to their Mr Potato Head.

Mr Banana, Mr Orange...!

You can have lots of fun by using the parts from Mr Potato Head on real fruit. For example, you might put the Mr Potato Head pieces into a banana, an orange, a cucumber, etc. It's always a good idea to take a photo of the finished product so that your child can share what they did with others! Your child might also like to re-name the game 'Mr Banana' or 'Mr Orange' and you can create lots of communication opportunities around asking what fruit or vegetable you should put each Mr Potato Head part in (the more parts you have, the more fun this is, because you can make a fruit (and vegetable) salad family with all the parts.

Mr Potato Head likes to hide

You can have lots of fun and create many communication opportunities by hiding all the parts to Mr Potato Head around the house and your child has to look for all the different parts and tell you where they found them. You can also turn it into a story (like the 'Spot' stories) where you take the potato with your child and look for all the parts and ask questions in Mr Potato Head's voice. For example, you might hold the potato and in a funny voice ask 'Are my eyes under the pillow?' and then your child looks under the pillow.

What's missing? What's different?

You can build Mr Potato Head with your child and then play a game where you take turns in closing your eyes while the other person changes something about Mr Potato Head and the other has to guess what is different and/or missing. You might need to help your child with this game if they are having trouble guessing by asking more specific questions (e.g. 'Is he missing his eyes or nose?').

BOOKS

All parents want their children to learn how to read, but books don't necessarily have to be about reading the words on the page. There are many 'pre' reading skills that children need to learn, such as looking at the pictures, turning the pages, etc. But in the early stages it is more important that your child enjoys books and playing different games with books. You can then move on to gradually focusing on the words.

Things to try

Books and torches

You can have lots of fun with books by using torches in the dark or under the blankets. Torches can create lots of communication opportunities such as requesting a turn (e.g. 'my turn') and introducing concepts such as 'on' and 'off'. Torches are also great with books because you can put a spotlight on the part of the picture that you want your child to look at and name the picture or simply follow the direction of the spotlight.

Funny voices

You can have lots of fun with your child by reading books in 'funny voices'. Your child might like you to pretend to be different characters from their favourite TV show or movie, or you might like to get their teddies out and put different voices on for each teddy.

You can also just do different things with your voice when reading books like whispering, croaking, squeaking, etc. and see how your child reacts.

Play it back!

If your child is unable to read the words in a book but likes to pretend they can, you might like to feed your child the lines from a book (e.g. you read a short sentence, and then they repeat after you while it is being recorded; then when you put it all together it is like an audio book but with your child's voice). Or your child might simply like to do sounds to the book (e.g. animal sounds, etc.).

Make it up!

Instead of reading a book word-for-word as it is written down, your child might like it more if you make up a story and include things that are important to them, like using their name in the story or names of friends or favourite TV characters. If they really like a story that you make up you might like to turn it into a book on the computer by typing the story and inserting pictures.

What's next...?

You can create lots of communication and guessing games around reading books by asking your child 'What happens next?' before turning the page over. If your child is having trouble guessing you might present them with two different options, for example

'Do you think it is a dog or snake on the next page?', or you might let them have a quick peek at what picture might be. This game works best when your child knows the book really well and can remember what might be in the pictures.

I spy in my little book...

'I spy with my little eye...' is a great game to play with picture books, because this encourages your child to look at everything in the picture. It is a good idea when starting out with the game initially to talk about all the things in the picture so that your child is familiar with all the names of the things that you might 'spy' with your little eye. If your child is having difficulty playing 'I spy' the original way (e.g. 'I spy... something that starts with the letter P') you might like to make it easier by saying 'I spy with my little eye something that is green' or you could use shapes, etc.

Microphones

Toy, real or pretend microphones can be great fun when reading a book, as you can take it in turns pretending to read or really reading the words in the book.

'Secret' bendy tube stories

Bendy tubes, like those found on vacuum cleaners (but you can get similar ones from the hardware/craft store) or cardboard tubes can be used to tell 'secret' stories.

For example, while reading a book to your child you can make it a 'secret' by talking into one end of the tube and placing the other end up to your child's ear. You can create lots of communication opportunities around whose turn it is to talk or listen, and decisions around whether your child wants to hold it up to their ear or mouth, etc.

PUZZLES AND SHAPE SORTERS

Puzzles and shape sorters are often the toys that we first introduce our children to when they are little. Many children with autism continue to like puzzles and shape sorters and enjoy the organization and routine of completing them. Often we use puzzles to teach independent play but you can also create lots of communication when using puzzles.

Things to try

Hide 'n' seek with the puzzle pieces

You can create lots of communication opportunities with puzzles by turning it into a hide 'n' seek game. For example, you could hide the pieces around the room and tell your child how many pieces they need to find, or you could turn it into a race with two puzzles and see who can find the puzzles pieces and complete the puzzle first. You might also like to play a game where they have to guess where the pieces are by asking you or by you telling them where to look (e.g. look inside the cup, under the box, behind the door).

Puzzle races

By using a timer you can have fun with your child by racing to finish puzzles. You might like to record/ chart your time and your child's and chat to them about trying to get a better time or who is quicker or slower at completing the puzzle.

Fishing for the puzzle

You can have fun with puzzle pieces by turning it into a fishing game. For example, by putting paper clips onto the puzzle pieces and placing them on the floor and making a fishing rod with a piece of dowel and attaching some string and a magnet to the end you can fish for the puzzle pieces. This is great for turn-taking and commenting about the pieces that each of you find on the end of your fishing rod.

Personal puzzles

Some children with autism aren't that motivated by puzzles, but will be if you make your own puzzle with a photo of a family member or a picture of a favourite character. Just attach the favourite picture to some cardboard, photocopy the picture (and use this as a back board) and cut the cardboard picture into various shapes for your child to then match to the photocopied back board.

Requesting and tricking

You can create lots of communication opportunities by mixing two lots of puzzle pieces together (start out with relatively easy puzzles) in a container and holding on to them and only giving your child the backboard of one puzzle. Present two pieces at a time and ask if your child wants piece A or piece B. You might intentionally present two items that you know don't fit into the puzzle, as this is a great game for teaching 'Yes, it fits' and 'No, it doesn't fit' or asking if they want a particular piece: 'Do you want the truck or the fire engine?'

DRAWING AND WRITING

Many parents are keen to get their children to learn to write. Some children with autism really like letters and numbers (sometimes this can be an obsession) and others don't care about them at all, but it *is* important in the early stages to create lots of opportunities to make drawing and writing fun. However, this doesn't just have to be about sitting at a table and tracing letters. For example, it doesn't matter if your child can't hold a pen properly or even draw or write, it's more about making marks on the page, or even the ground, and having fun with it.

Things to try

Chalk and water painting

Chalk drawing and using water and a paintbrush to draw are great activities for encouraging your child to learn to draw and write, particularly if your child likes to spend most of their time outdoors. You can create lots of communication opportunities by holding onto the chalk and getting your child to ask for different colours of chalk, or you could take turns with them in drawing and they could tell you what they want you to draw (which is particularly helpful if they are not good at drawing). Simply by filling a bucket or container with water and using paintbrushes to dip in the water, you and your child can do water painting, which is great to do on pavements or on a fence.

Trains and cars

Many children with autism 'love' trains and cars, and you can turn this into a drawing and writing activity by simply encouraging your child to move the trains/ cars in a tray of sand, flour or paint. By doing this you can create patterns, shapes and words with their wheels. You can also do the same with little toys/ figures such as dinosaurs, figurines from children's cartoons and movies, and so on, by dragging or walking them through the sand, flour or paint.

Food writing

You can create some fun and mess by writing and drawing with different foods. By using lots of different coloured condiments, sauces and sweet toppings (e.g. ice-cream toppings and jams) and putting them in different squeezy bottles you can draw lots of different things, either on food or on a placemat or tray (you don't always have to eat your creation, although you child might like to!). Funny faces are fun to draw, so are balloons, animals and squiggles and shapes.

Playdough™ drawing and writing

Lots of children with autism really like the texture of playdough, and when you roll it into long thin snakes you can manipulate it into different letters, numbers and shapes. Or you can roll the playdough to make it into a thin flat surface and use a plastic knife or fork to draw or write in it. Lots of choices can be encouraged through colours, numbers, letters, pictures and shapes.

Line chasers

Line chasers are small toy cars that have an infra-red laser underneath the bottom of the car which 'magically' follows the lines that your child has drawn. This is a great toy for motivating your child to learn to make basic lines or learn to write.

Light and laser writing

Torches and laser pens can be used to 'draw' or 'write' on walls or ceilings, or to trace over chalk letters on the ground. This can help your child to watch and follow or copy what you are doing, and this can contribute to a great game in the dark, in tents or under the duvet!

Computer writing

Computers often have drawing or writing programs built into them. You can make pictures by inserting different shapes or have fun with colours, patterns/ effects, and sizes/width of lines. If your child has difficulty using a computer you can create lots of communication opportunities by getting them to point or ask for what they want and for you to draw it on the computer. Your child might also like some of the animations and sounds that you can add to the pictures/shapes (e.g. they can fly in from the side, flash or make a 'zoom' sound as they appear on the screen).

Shaving cream/foam

As mentioned in Chapter 4, by spreading a thin layer of shaving cream or foam in a tray or on a tabletop you can encourage your child to use their finger or a paintbrush to draw or write in the shaving cream (your child might prefer to wear gloves if they don't like getting their hands dirty). You can keep drawing over and over again by simply smoothing the cream/foam back over. You can also use foods such as custard or yoghurt and you get the same effect (but watch out as it can get messy!).

Whiteboard drawing

Whiteboards attached to walls or mini, portable whiteboards can be used to draw on and wipe away. You can create lots of opportunities for play and games with whiteboards such as drawing a picture (e.g. a dog) and getting your child to close their eyes while you wipe away a particular part (e.g. the tail) and have your child guess what you wiped away or have them try to re-draw it!

Toys to buy or try

There are lots of toys in the shops that can be used to motivate your child to draw or write – in particular, toys such as Magna Doodle™, Aqua Draw™, Etch A Sketch™, Spirograph™, magic pens/markers and scented markers are often enjoyed by children with autism.

COMPUTER AND ELECTRONIC GAMES

Most children with autism really enjoy computers and electronic games – in fact, a little too much sometimes. Generally speaking, computers and electronic games are not a very social thing to do with your child and don't allow for a lot of communication opportunities to occur. However, with some thought and careful planning you can create communication opportunities while using computers. Choosing the right game to support commnication opportunities is important. For example, try to use games that are educational but fun and with which your child needs help (as they are therefore forced to communicate with you to ask for help). Or, use a game that has natural short starts and stops in it whereby you can introduce turn-taking.

Also, try to set boundaries with the computer and think carefully what you are using the computer for. Is it a reward for doing something good (where you might let your child have uninterrupted 'play' for a specified time), or are you wanting to use it as an educational tool to encourage communication (and by means of which you will be interacting more with your child)?

Things to try

Time and tell

It is important to limit your child's time on the computer, particularly if your child is getting obsessed with it. This will help your child to learn to start and finish a turn and also to share the computer with other people. First of all, it is important to choose a timer that your child can best understand – this might be a sand timer, a clock that has a coloured wedge that gets smaller as the time counts down, a digital timer, a ticking kitchen timer or a token board where the tokens are taken away as the time passes. It is then important to set the timer with your child and explain that they have a limited amount of time and to set their expectations for when the timer is finished. To create more communication opportunities, you can encourage your child to tell you what they did after each turn on the computer (which can be a good skill for telling personal stories).

Switches

Sometimes computer games will be too complex for your child to play. However, it is possible to make some games simpler by attaching a switch device to them. These are available from www.inclusivetic.com Switches are generally just a big button that your child can press for the next event to occur on the computer. Another idea is to attach a sticker to the mouse button/space bar and to set up programs on PowerPoint™ whereby your child just presses the sticker for the next action to occur. (If you do not know how to do this, make friends with someone who is good at computers and they will be able to help set this up for you!)

Chat book show

You can create lots of communication opportunities by inserting personal photos that relate to your child (e.g. like a 'chat book' or an 'about me' book) in a 'show and tell' slide presentation. This will give your child an opportunity to press the buttons on the computer and for them to comment and share news about themselves with other people sitting around the computer. If your child is shy or has trouble verbally telling stories you might like to pre-record the talking onto the computer (either you or your child) and your child can press the button for the pictures to appear and then press the button for the audio to begin.

Story book alive!

Similar to the 'chat book shows', if your child has a book that they really like (or which you would like them to be more interested in!) you can re-create the story on the computer using a slide-show program. By inserting pictures, sounds/audio, words, animations, etc. you can help your child present the story to you or their friends. *The Very Hungry Caterpillar* by Eric Carle is a great book to re-create on the computer.

Click and do!

If your child enjoys using a computer you might like to use it to help your child to learn how to follow more complex instructions. You could make up a slide presentation whereby each slide has an instruction that your child has to follow (similar to 'Simon Says'). For example, you might have a slide that has written, audio and/or animated pictures that tells your child to do ten claps and then three jumps. Your child can press the button on the computer to see what you and your child have to do next.

Google Images

You can create lots of opportunities for requesting and commenting by searching for pictures online, via software such as Google Images. Your child can ask you to find pictures of various animals or characters from their favourite movie or TV show. If your child is having trouble generating ideas for pictures that they want to search for you might like to help out by having some DVD covers close by or a toy catalogue. You might like to print the pictures out and put them up around the house, so your child can talk about them later.

Drawing on the computer

Computers often have drawing or writing programs built into them. You can make pictures by inserting different shapes or having fun with colours, patterns/ effects, and sizes/width of lines. If your child has difficulty using a computer you can create lots of communication opportunities by getting them to point or ask for what they want and for you to draw it on the computer. Your child might also like some of the animations and sounds that you can add to the pictures/shapes (e.g. flying in from the side, flashing or making a 'zoom' sound as they appear on the screen).

Wii™, Playstation™, Xbox™

There are a lot of new electronic game systems in the shops that encourage multiple players and provide more opportunities for communication. For example, Wii tennis can be a fun game to play with your child as you can stop regularly to comment about who is winning and who made a good shot, etc! There are many good games out on the market – just try to think how you might be able to incorporate some communication within the game. It is easier to insert the communication opportunities when they first start playing the game so they just assume that you stopping and starting the game and talking to them is all part of the game!

APPENDIX 1:
RECORD SHEETS

THE IMPORTANCE OF RECORDING

It is helpful to record how your child reacts to various toys, foods, games and social activities because this will give you ideas about which items/activities you need to start your child off with when helping them learn to communicate. When you record how your child reacts to various items you will start to see themes or patterns of things that they like – for example, things that move, things that are crunchy, things that are yellow, etc. This will in turn give you more ideas of things to try with your child. Also, by encouraging other people who are involved with your child to do the same you might begin to learn that your child likes different things in different environments and with different people. It is also helpful to show this list to your occupational therapist or speech and language therapist as they might also be able to give you ideas about how you can extend these activities.

RECORD SHEET

Child's Name _____ Date _____

Item/Activity	How was it used?	Child's reaction	Child's level of communication	Ideas for trying next time! (similar item or using item/activity in different way)
Example: Normal balloon blown up and tied	Example: Played with the balloon by hitting it up	Example: Happy, smiling	Example: Reaching for item with arm and when taken away verbally requested 'more balloon'	Example: 1. Drawing a face on a balloon (because he likes labelling face parts) 2. Rocket balloons (he likes things that are noisy) 3. Blowing up brown paper bags and popping them

APPENDIX 2:
TRIED AND TESTED RESOURCES

A LIST OF GREAT TOYS AND RESOURCES THAT WE USE

Throughout the book we have tried to avoid using specific brand names of items, wherever possible. However, if you are interested in finding these items sometimes it is helpful to have a specific brand name – for example, when searching the internet.

Marble Run (Early Learning Centre or GALT)

Mr Potato Head

Koosh balls

Rocket balloons

Popoids™

Flying disk balloon

Stix and Bricks™

Pop Up Pirate™

Scented felt-tip pens

Springy Spiders (Early Learning Centre)

Magic pens (Hamleys)

Viewmasters

Wind-up toys

Light chasers (Disney and other brands)

Pull-back cars

Scented bubbles

Playdough

Touchable bubbles

Potty putty

Light-up spinners

Magnetic building sets

Vibrating toys

Whiteboard and dry wipe pens

Piece of stretchy Lycra 2metre square

Pound a Ball

Noisy shape-sorter (a shape-sorter that groans when you put the right shape in the hole)

Frog in a box (GALT)

USEFUL READING

Books on communication

Frost, L.A. and Bondy, A.S. (2002) *The Picture Exchange Communication System: Training Manual* (2nd edn). Newark, DE: Pyramid Educational Products.

Gray, C. (1994) *The Social Storybook.* Arlington, TX: Future Horizons.

Hodgdon, A.L. (1995) *Visual Strategies for Improving Communication: Practical Supports for School and Home.* Troy, MI: Quirk Roberts.

McClannahan, L.E. and Krantz, P.J. (1999) *Activity Schedules for Children with Autism: Teaching Independent Behaviors.* Bethesda, MD: Woodbine House.

Quill, K. (1995) *Teaching Children with Autism: Strategies to Enhance Communication and Socialization.* New York, NY: Delmar.

Quill, K. (2000) *Do, Watch, Listen, Say: Social and Communication Intervention for Children with Autism.* Baltimore, MD: Paul H. Brookes.

Sussman, F. (1999) *More than Words: Helping Parents Promote Communication and Social Skills in Children with Autistic Spectrum Disorders.* Toronto, Ontario: The Hanen Centre.

Sussman, F. (2006) *TalkAbility: People Skills for Verbal Children on the Autism Spectrum – A Guide for Parents.* Toronto, Ontario: The Hanen Centre.

Books on sensory issues

Biel, L. and Peske, N. (2005) *Raising a Sensory Smart Child: The Definitive Handbook for Helping your Child with Sensory Integration Issues.* New York, NY: Penguin Group.

Heller, S. (2002) *Too Loud Too Bright Too Fast Too Tight: What to Do if You are Sensory Defensive in an Overstimulating World.* New York, NY: HarperCollins.

Kranowitz, C. (2003) *The Out of Sync Child has Fun: Activities for Kids with Sensory Processing Disorder.* York, NY: Penguin Group.

Kranowitz, C. (2005) *The Out of Sync Child: Recognizing and Coping with Sensory Processing Disorder.* New York, NY: Penguin Group.

Miller, L. (2006) *Sensational Kids: Hope and Help for Children with Sensory Processing Disorder (SPD).* New York, NY: Penguin Group.

Yack, E., Aquilla, P. and Sutton, S. (2002) *Building Bridges Through Sensory Integration: Therapy for Children with Autism and Other Pervasive Developmental Disorders* (2nd edn). Las Vegas, NV: Sensory Resources.

General books on autism

Attwood, T. (2008) *The Complete Guide to Asperger's Syndrome.* London, UK: Jessica Kingsley Publishers.

Bondy, A. and Sulzer-Azaroff, S. (2002) *The Pyramid Approach to Education in Autism.* Newark, DE: Pyramid Educational Products.

Hodgdon, A.L. (1999) *Solving Behavior Problems in Autism: Improving Communication with Visual Strategies.* Troy, MI: Quirk Roberts.

Maurice, C. (ed.), Green, G. and Luce, S. (co-eds) (1996) *Behavioral Intervention for Young Children with Autism: A Manual for Parents and Professionals.* Austin, TX: ProEd.

Notbohm, E. (2005) *Ten Things Every Child with Autism Wishes You Knew.* Arlington, TX: Future Horizons.

Offit, P. (2008) *Autism's False Prophets: Bad Science, Risky Medicine, and the Search for a Cure.* New York, NY: Columbia University Press.

Siegel, B. (2007) *Helping Children with Autism Learn: Treatment Approaches for Parents and Professionals.* New York, NY: Oxford University Press.

Szatmari, P. (2004) *A Mind Apart: Understanding Children with Autism and Asperger Syndrome.* New York, NY: Guilford Press.

AUTISM ORGANIZATIONS AND USEFUL WEBSITES

www.autism-resources.com

This site provides information and links regarding autism and Asperger's syndrome.

www.awares.org

This organization provides a directory of information and list of resources, both online and offline, in Wales and worldwide.

www.hanen.org

This is a Canadian based organization that provides a wide range of programmes and resources to support parents and professionals to help their children to develop communication skills.

www.nas.org.uk

The National Autistic Society is a UK based organization that supports the rights and interests of people with autism and their families.

www.out-of-sync-child.com

This website provides resources and activities for children with sensory processing issues.

www.pecs.com

This organization provides information about training, consultation and support to parents, carers and professionals involved with children and adults with communication difficulties.

www.positivelyautism.com

This website provides a free online magazine designed to discuss issues and positive stories about autism. The website is designed for parents, teachers, individuals with autism, and other members of the autism community.

www.raisingchildren.net.au/children_with_autism

This website is part of a larger Australian government initiative to help parents make decisions about their children. This particular site provides easy to understand information about autism and provides information to help parents make informed decisions about their child with autism.

INDEX OF EQUIPMENT